Columbia University

Contributions to Education

Teachers College Series

No. 887

AMS PRESS
NEW YORK

An Experiment in Modifying Attitudes toward the Negro

By

FRED TREDWELL SMITH

SUBMITTED IN PARTIAL FULFILLMENT OF THE REQUIREMENTS
FOR THE DEGREE OF DOCTOR OF PHILOSOPHY IN THE
FACULTY OF PHILOSOPHY, COLUMBIA UNIVERSITY

*Published with the Approval of
Professor Helen M. Walker, Sponsor*

BUREAU OF PUBLICATIONS

Teachers College, Columbia University

NEW YORK · 1943

Library of Congress Cataloging in Publication Data

Smith, Fred Tredwell, 1894-
    An experiment in modifying attitudes toward the
Negro.

    Reprint of the 1943 ed., issued in series: Teachers
College, Columbia University. Contributions to educa-
tion, no. 887.
    Originally presented as the author's thesis,
Columbia.
    Bibliography: p.
    1. Negroes. 2. United States--Race question.
3. Attitude change. I. Title. II. Series: Columbia
University. Teachers College. Contributions to educa-
tion, no. 887.
E185.61.S63 1972   301.15'43'30145196073 76-177777
ISBN 0-404-55887-9

From the edition of 1943 , New York
First AMS edition published in 1972
Manufactured in the United States

AMS PRESS, INC.
NEW YORK, N. Y.   10003

". . . the work of adjusting to American life the various color and national groups and of adjusting American life to them is still of primary importance."

From *Recent Social Trends in the United States*

Foreword

IN THE world struggle for democracy, of which our own national life is a phase, the instruments of science can play a critical role; for they can establish clear verification of guiding hypotheses and assay the effects of democratically oriented programs. F. Tredwell Smith's application of a carefully planned experimental method in a procedure for developing Negro-white understanding has an immense importance. It demonstrates a measurably huge result from a relatively short period of race contacts under conditions so well controlled as to force the conclusion that these specific experiences are in fact important specific factors in the amelioration of race relations. Secondly, it reveals a large transfer value from one situation to another; amelioration produced in visits to cultural centers in Harlem have a *generalized* effect upon attitudes toward Negroes. In the face of so much defeatist talk about the weakness of scientific method in a complex cultural setting, an insightful and technically masterful answer is given in this ocular demonstration.

The author would be the last to conclude that this single approach is "the solution" of our race problems. The reading of this specific study will make clear enough that in an issue so complex and so vital to democracy, we need all the science, all the humanity, all the vision we can get.

GARDNER MURPHY

Author's Preface

WHEN THE experiment reported here was being conducted, conscious interest in interracial adjustments tended to be confined to special circles. Now world war, in polarizing for millions other basic human issues, sharpens this one also on a world scale. At one pole is the Nazi philosophy of racial contempt and limitless exploitation. On our side experience of our need for participation by the colored millions at home and abroad, if early victory in the uncertain conflict is to be secured, favors correction of old inequalities and accelerates changes in traditional relations. Simultaneously the colored peoples of the earth move toward achieving fuller rights. Moreover, a consciousness is spreading that unless victory is to be hollow, the world after the war must proceed more rapidly in the direction of ethnic democracy. Education may well be much more actively concerned with these perspectives in the future than in the past and be called upon for greater contributions to these adjustments. The modification of attitudes toward a group such as the Negro becomes therefore a significant problem for education to-day. Consequently the publication of this experiment now may well be more timely than earlier.

The writer's indebtedness should be acknowledged to the many individuals who gave generously of their time, counsel, and abilities in making this experiment possible. In particular to the many representative Negro leaders who extended their hospitality and their talents to the program of the Harlem Seminar, sincere thanks are due. Their aid was crucial.

Special acknowledgment is made to Dr. Gardner Murphy, Chairman of the Department of Psychology of the College of

the City of New York, whose keen sense of vital problems calling for solution to-day and exact knowledge of the state of research first confirmed the writer in his enterprise, and whose
deft initial advice helped safeguard it from pitfalls; also to the
Reverend Shelton Bishop, rector of St. Philip's Episcopal
Church of Harlem, whose educational and social insight and intimate knowledge of his community were given without stint
in helping arrange the Seminar experiences; to Dr. Harrison
Elliott of Union Theological Seminary, and Dr. Percival Symonds and Dr. Ralph Spence of Teachers College, who individually and collectively as dissertation committee responded
repeatedly with expert advice; and especially to Dr. Helen
Walker, sponsor of the dissertation, whose critical judgment
and keen interest in the problem have benefited the outcome at
innumerable points and who lent to the enterprise her steady
and careful concern; finally to Dr. Randolph B. Smith, Director
of the Little Red Schoolhouse in New York City, brother of the
writer, whose professional judgment and research experience
meant much to the study from its inception.

F. T. S.

Contents

Contents

An Experiment in Modifying
Attitudes toward the Negro

I: Introduction—Improvement of Negro–White Relationships an Educational Responsibility

THE Negro problem in the United States is of admitted interest and importance. Changing form from decade to decade and century to century it continues to present American destiny with a great question mark. Politically, economically, socially, culturally, Negroes condition the evolution of America in countless ways, obvious or devious, recognized or unobserved. Doubtless this problem is one item only in that vast congeries of worldwide problems, economic and cultural at bottom, which center around the concept of race. Yet it has a dramatic character of its own which has attracted general human attention.

Implicit in the problem, and one function of its changing aspect, are the attitudes of white Americans toward the Negro. Put thus, it is no doubt a commonplace. But not so common is the realization that prevalent attitudes of the dominant race, by restricting opportunities to earn a livelihood, to gain an education, to receive social services, and to enjoy the advances of civilization, have stark social effects. While it is always precarious to distribute responsibility among social causes, the concentration of American illiteracy in the Negro South (to take one example) and the marked retardation of Southern Negro children in Northern schools seem in part connected with Southern white attitudes toward financial support of Negro schools, length of the school year, compensation of teachers, and enforcement of school attendance (5:VI).*

---

* Initial numbers refer to serially numbered sources in the Bibliography (p. 127); other numbers to chapter and page.

Similarly the markedly higher death rate of Negroes North and South—"the Negro death rates are almost half again as high as the whites" (21:583)—is not unreasonably related in a degree to difficulties met by Negroes in getting a living: the tradition of disparagement in industry, the necessity of beginning at the bottom regardless of skill, friction in labor troubles, effective "dead lines" in the South, the need of overcoming stereotypes of executives regarding their traits and abilities (21:581, 2), and the decidedly higher incidence of the burden of unemployment. As Dewey says of racial discrimination in another connection, "The situation then produces conditions which justify the belief in respective superiority and inferiority. For of course any people held in subjection and at great disadvantage economically and politically is bound to show the consequences." (7:8)

In addition to objective social costs of discrimination there are of course psychological and emotional burdens of the sort now being reflected increasingly in Negro arts and letters. To sum up a vast field of social investigation, one can say that in the pursuit of American objectives of democracy and equality of opportunity in life many common American attitudes toward the Negro stand squarely across the road.

Whatever strategy is contemplated today in dealing with this situation has to reckon with significant recent developments in the American Negro world. Negro migration to the North and West, for instance, which added nearly a half million to those sections between 1910 and 1920, and nearly a further million between 1920 and 1930 (21:566) is rapidly "whitening" the rural South, and creating or enlarging Negro colonies in the urban North. Negro-white adjustments are increasingly more of national, less of merely sectional, concern. In spite of obstacles, Negroes have made their way into industry, the semiskilled and skilled trades, and the professions in significant numbers. The Negro middle class continues to develop, and in the arts Negro representation is rapidly increasing. With the spread of higher education, the character of Negro leadership has gradually changed, shifting influence in the community "from the uneducated preachers to the educated preachers, the teachers, and the business men" (21:589).

In short, it is a different Negro America which orients itself in the midst of white America at the present time, different geographically, industrially, socially, and intellectually, from that which existed when prevailing white attitudes toward the Negro arose. Yet while immediate contacts have aroused in new quarters new antagonisms or new appreciations, or reduced old ones, among the majority of whites a lag in awareness and in adjustment to the changed conditions persists. For a group suffering from the isolation of "social distance" this lack of awareness by the dominant group constitutes another of its prevailing handicaps. At the same time the situation presents to education definite and specific tasks.

So far, however, as prejudice is an ingredient in American attitudes toward the Negro, one is forced to go deeper. What is the nature of race prejudice? Dewey in a penetrating and succinct analysis, originally addressed to Chinese intellectuals, accounts for it as follows. Like prejudice in general it is not that irrationality which consists in an incomplete use of reason, but obedience to instinct and habit which is "the fundamental sort of irrationality, for it supplies the *cause* of our defective reasoning." (Italics not in original.) "It is a desire or emotion which makes us see things in a particular light and gives a slant to all our beliefs" (7:2).

Though eventually overlain by many other elements, the universal prejudice against the strange is, according to Dewey, the foundation upon which these other elements rest for their efficacy. The anti-strange feeling left to itself tends to disappear under normal conditions, as what was strange becomes familiar, but persistent physical differences which do not wear off and which continue therefore to accentuate the fact of being strange, an intruder, and a potential invader, provide something concrete, tangible, visible, to react against. Marked cultural differences function in a similar manner. While ordinarily we learn to associate mental and moral traits with an individual person and do not generalize a particular unpleasant or pleasant experience, but individualize it and connect it with him personally, in the case of a member of a strange group we are not so likely to individualize it. Political domination in turn changes race prejudice into racial discrimination, and increases the handicaps of those held in subjection, while it fosters arrogance and contempt among the dominant group. Finally the economic factor—competition, exploitation, differences in standard of living, etc.—contributes the most rational impetus in the confirming of national animosities. "Scientifically, the concept of race is largely a fiction, but as designating a whole group of actual phenomena it is a practical reality" (7:12).

From this analysis it is worth while to single out certain points for emphasis, for instance, the irrational and emotional elements in race prejudice, the intricate tangle of historical and social factors, failure through social distance or group conflict for familiarity with the strange to be carried to completion, interruption of the process of individualization and the formation of racial stereotypes, finally the grim facts of political and economic conflict. When in addition it is realized that apart from or prior to the influence of these factors in a child's history a prejudiced group can transmit its attitudes early to its children by social conditioning, we have a sufficient description of the phenomenon for our present purpose (14). The basic result is a low valuation attached to the group discriminated against and a low sense of worth for its individual members.

Before raising the eventual question whether attitudes toward the Negro can be changed, it is well to ask how significant in the whole strategy of bettering race relations would an improvement in individual attitudes be. It requires little reflection to realize the limited freedom of the individual in the face of mass custom and the replenishing of racial antagonism in the masses from vast underlying clashes in political and economic interest. As Dewey says:

> . . . the cultivated person who thinks that what is termed racial friction will disappear if other persons only attain his own state of enlightenment misjudges the whole situation. . . . Individuals here and there achieve freedom from prejudice and rational control of instinctive bias with comparative ease, but the mass cannot attain it until there has been a change not only in education and in the means of publicity, but also in political and industrial organization (7:15).

This kind of difficulty is of course a common one for education, and to the extent that education is regarded as a means for the progressive adjustment of society to its stresses and strains, may be considered normal. Gradually accumulating shifts in attitude alone make possible fundamental adjustments, and to these shifts many influences contribute. The main question is: what measures can education rely on to be effective?

A vast deal of effort has been, and is being, expended by a great variety of organizations, groups, and individuals in the effort to improve attitudes toward the Negro, and a valuable body of experience has been worked out. The whole story would be kaleidoscopic. The areas, auspices, policies, methods of these undertakings are legion. Sometimes the educational aim has been central, sometimes merely ancillary to other purposes. Adult education in many forms, the education of children, community adjustment of cases of racial conflict or injustice by the use of public opinion, local civic service and action, student activities and studies, are a few of the areas. National and local church bodies, student Young Men's and Young Women's Christian Associations, interracial commissions, university departments, and other academic authorities, have been representative auspices. Methods have included in their range

Negro concerts and art exhibits, and sociological investigations of Negro housing and labor. Outstanding in leading Southern opinion since the World War has been the work of the Southern Interracial Commission; significant nationally among present and former college students has been the influence of the student Young Men's and Young Women's Christian Associations, particularly through their summer conferences; and in a few˙ central cities International Houses and so-called "Friendship" and "Reconciliation Trips" have had a pioneering role in supplying cultural contacts for special groups with individuals and circles of Negro society. In the field of political and legal rights the National Association for the Advancement of Colored People has enlisted the interest of many individuals of prominence, and the National Urban League has contributed to a greater concern of social workers and others with Negro housing, health, employment, and public services in the cities. These are only a few of the many agencies deserving special mention. An admirable critical study by Paul E. Baker analyzes the principal movements (28).*

From a welter of measures now employed in these enterprises the deliberate use of cultural contacts with individuals and groups of Negroes of marked talent or achievement seems especially interesting and promising in affecting attitudes. Many people look back to personal contacts of this sort supplied at conferences, at schools, or in visits to Negro centers as influential in their own development. On the other hand, others, white and Negro, feel a very definite skepticism. By hearsay, as onlookers, or as active participants, they know of these visits, meetings, discussions, conferences, and have their doubts about the value of the time and money involved. It must be admitted that these doubts are particularly insistent among exactly those Negro leaders and participants who, because their co-operation

---

* In recent years the efforts of various labor organizations have been outstanding both in range and in measure of success.

is essential, frequently have to bear the brunt of the burden. Moreover, the doors of America's Harlems swing *in* more readily than they swing *out*, and reciprocity in many areas of co-operation is infrequent. Do these contacts "accomplish" anything— "do any good"?

An experiment in modifying attitudes toward the Negro through such cultural contacts should prove of value. More particularly, an experiment attempting scientific measurement of certain of these supposed changes in attitudes would seem to be especially pertinent. If nothing apparent is immediately accomplished by these means, the various undertakings, non-academic, semi-academic, or academic, using them can question whether they should be supplanted, extended and intensified, or regarded simply as ground-breaking for a more distant future. If on the contrary the experiment seems to reveal positive accomplishment in the direction of an improvement in race attitudes, toward increased tolerance and fairmindedness, not only will present efforts be encouraged, but a definite directive may be given to academic education.

Modern philosophies of education argue for the inclusion of experiential values in the student's personal curriculum. Sociology is emphasizing the need for first-hand social experience to serve as a reference point of concrete imagery for thinking and acting in a world necessarily described in abstract terms and characterized increasingly by non-face-to-face relationships (8). In academic administration a new philosophy of the curriculum is encouraging greater flexibility and assistance in practical arrangements for experience beyond university walls. A tradition of travel to urban centers is beginning in rural colleges, and a deliberate use of the metropolitan environment is on its way in those centrally located. If experience of the cultural life and activities of Negro society proves a valuable contribution to American interracial adjustments, the swiftest mode of advance is by education of the leaders and educators of the public.

The experiment then will be shaped with one eye on its practicability for an academic environment. It will be short, but not too short, it will have a certain continuity, progressive development, Gestalt. It will appeal to intelligence without being intellectualistic; it will allow for the elements of habit and emotion in attitude. It will therefore not be comprehensive; it will definitely select pleasurable experiences. It will be adapted to individualize personalities among the Negro group by exposing students to vividly contrasting persons of ability possessing a variety of talents, interests, appearances, and views. Fundamentally it will seek to enhance the valuation put upon individual Negroes and the Negro group as a whole by direct experience of the quality of mind, attainment, and outlook of outstanding individuals and groups, on the principle that the estimate of value and capacity of a group actually proceeds that way, just as the value of mankind in general is measured, by a Plato, a Beethoven, or a Saint Francis of Assisi, rather than by the mediocre and unawakened. After all there is a tacit assumption that part of education consists in acquaintance with men and society.

The experiment, in short, will be an attempt to measure scientifically the effectiveness of a particular type of educational procedure in producing favorable modifications in attitudes toward the Negro.

II: Previous Research on the Problem
of Modifying Attitudes

No scientific experiment to the writer's knowledge has been undertaken to measure changes in attitude toward the Negro induced by contacts with cultured Negro society. Research in its immediate bearing on the problem radiates out from other types of experimentation upon these attitudes, to reports on other racial attitudes and suggestions of possibly correlated factors, on to the broad and rapidly expanding field of research into attitudes and opinions as a whole. In addition there are recent contributions to the logic and technique of attitude study.

Excellent critical surveys by Murphy (17), Bain from a somewhat different standpoint (2), the Department of Superintendence of the National Education Association in its Tenth Yearbook on "Character Education" (18), and Watson (26) sum up the wider field and incorporate outstanding references covered in earlier summaries by Allport and Vernon (1), May, Hartshorne, and Welty (16), and others. Except for a few subsequent or unpublished books and articles they serve as comprehensive guides to the field. Abstracts in the Tenth Yearbook bring together much scattered material in very handy form. It may be noted in passing that the present experiment was conceived during perusal of Murphy's *Experimental Social Psychology* by the relative paucity of experiments undertaken to produce changes in attitude and by Murphy's remark that "The crying need for research on Negro-white antagonisms has . . . resulted as yet in very little exact research." (17:639)*

* No attempt has been made to cover the large body of literature that has appeared since this pioneer experiment was put into form. Readers may consult the second edition of *Experimental Social Psychology* by Gardner Murphy and Theo-

Beginning with investigations bearing directly on attitudes toward the Negro, it is scarcely necessary to underline the obvious fact that Negroes are out toward the extreme of social distance compared with many racial and national groups. This is an interesting aspect of a number of studies involving indication of rank-order preferences for different groups. Bogardus with 248 students found the Turk at the bottom, the Negro next to the bottom; 178 Jews put the Negro at the bottom (17:631). Young, reporting on the race prejudice of 450 undergraduates at the University of Pennsylvania, found the rank of the Negro just above that of the Mexican, the latter being the lowest in a series of twenty-four racial and national groups ranked according to supposed inborn ability. A course on American race problems, which might have been expected to destroy the belief in race differences in inborn ability, had little or no effect. Two percent of 211 students at the beginning of the first term stated that there were no mental differences permitting such classification (an optional answer under the test), and only two percent at the close. The second term, in a class of 224 containing more Negroes and Jews, the proportion refusing to attempt a rank listing was 11 percent at the beginning, and 19 percent at the end. Rank order correlation of 20 nationalities before and after the course was .98 the first term and .96 the second. Young concludes that students' racial opinions and biases have been formed over a period of years by means which leave a more lasting impression than formal lectures or assignments (18:143-4, Study No. 62). Schlorff (22) in a valuable unpublished study to be discussed later developed a social distance scale by paired comparisons on Thurstone's lines among high school students of Hoboken. On this scale 425 students of the same (cosmopolitan) population rated the Negro lowest of all those groups with whom they had had contacts, and only slightly above the

dore Newcomb, and the unpublished "Digest of Books and Articles on Prejudices and Education for Overcoming Prejudices" by Genevieve Chase and Otto Klineberg in mimeographed form (December, 1940).

Turk, Japanese, Hindu, and Chinese. All five were barely tolerated in the capacity of "citizen" on the scale and failed to reach the next level of "fellow pupil never addressed." The same order obtained with a smaller experimental and control group. (22:28a)

The well-known difference in French and English cultural patterns in these matters has been experimentally indicated by Lapiere by a sampling questionnaire addressed to "the man in the street." In the course of casual acquaintance with people of many walks of life he inquired their willingness to admit a Negro to residence in their house or establishment. Classifying as "doubtful" some thoughtful persons who tried to pass deliberate judgment and to weigh the various factors involved, he found the following contrast: England—without prejudice 14, doubtful 47, with prejudice 254, total 315; France—without prejudice 287, doubtful 96, with prejudice 45, total 428. Excluding data obtained from the upper group in France, where cases of prejudice seemed to be the expression of "social status," and from two towns which showed abnormal conditions, totals for France show—without prejudice 279, doubtful 72, and with prejudice 9, total 360 (18:147, Study No. 67). It is an interesting speculation whether or not the attitude toward the Negro in the American South today would be the same or different if this region had been colonized from France instead of England, and if Frenchmen instead of Anglo-Saxons had administered its slave economy.

The influence of contrasting cultural patterns of the North and South is evident in a study by Hunter (13). Choosing New York City and North Carolina as the areas where race relations of the respective sections were presumably at their best, she addressed questionnaires to eight groups, a white church congregation and a Negro church congregation and a white college and a Negro college in North Carolina, and corresponding groups in New York City. The questionnaires were scored so that higher scores indicated more goodwill. The results with the white groups showed a gradation in means and medians as follows: Columbia College students first, followed by Northern adults, University of North Carolina students, and Southern adults, the means being respectively 67.26, 53.27, 49.00, 40.07. A sharp sectional difference of opinion was found upon the following issues: approving title Mr., Mrs., and Miss; eating with a Negro; disapproving the Jim Crow car; approving equal pay; disapproving restriction of the suffrage. No sectional difference of opinion was found upon the following issues: rating Negro intelligence at more than 50 percent of the intelligence of whites (in no group did as many as half assent!); approving college education for Negroes (high agreement) ; disapproving segregation (all low: percents 9, 3, 5, and 4 respectively) ; disapproving term "nigger," not ranking all Negroes alike, disapproving lynching (all high agreement). The issue which showed the largest sectional difference concerned the question of eating with a Negro. Differences between the Southern university and the Northern adult group were in the main relatively small in comparison with the difference between the Southern university and the Southern adult group, which suggests a reconditioning effect as the result of education. A sharp *racial* clash is revealed over the issue of segregation, which is given by the Negro groups as the chief cause of Negro antipathy, since this is the issue upon which the whites stand most closely together on the one hand and the Negroes most closely together on the other. Underrating the intelligence of the Negro, another cause of friction, is shown when 19 percent of the Northern college group, 30 percent of the Southern college group, 44 percent of the Northern adults, and 63 percent of the Southern adults say the Negro is only 25 percent as intelligent as the white man. It will be noted that higher education seemed to temper antipathy. Though Hunter points out that the number of cases in her study were small, her results are suggestive.

Sectional differences in scores on tests using somewhat the same questions as Hunter were found by Likert between Northern and Southern groups (15). His investigation, which bears on problems of measurement, will be discussed below.

That the effect of Southern cultural patterns can be and is being overcome in individual cases is indicated by another questionnaire study by Collins (18:42, 3, Study No. 60). A brief questionnaire on racial attitudes sent to a number of white Southerners brought 50 replies. Answers indicated that most of those replying could be called unprejudiced. Thirty-eight items were listed with instructions to underline those felt to have been most important in overcoming the individual's prejudice. Thirty-four men marked Christian Association summer conferences; 29, Christian Association secretaries; 29, Negro students; 28, visiting speakers; 24, Christian Association discussion groups; 23, white friends; 22, Negro poetry; 22, Negro professional people; 20, injustice witnessed. Among less frequently mentioned influences were Negro novels, Negro journals, and Negro servants.

A much more elaborate and finely discriminating analysis of possible factors associated with change of attitudes is contained in a questionnaire by Baker entitled "A Study in the Change of Race Attitudes Before, During, and After College" and addressed to a nation-wide group of several hundred persons who are known to have changed their attitudes toward the Negro markedly. The results of this questionnaire are incorporated in Baker's study already mentioned (28). Ten or eleven specific factors are suggested under each of the following general influences: personal contacts, learning about Negroes, participation in race-co-operative activities, and work on behalf of Negroes without Negro participation. Biographical information, including personal classification of one's earlier attitude and the nature and rate of change, is also recorded.

Another group of studies represents various attempts to induce more favorable attitudes toward the Negro among high school students. The use of assemblies in high schools of Philadelphia, under the direction of Mrs. Rachel Davis Du Bois, to present the cultural achievements of Negroes and other races has been extensive, but no measurement of its effectiveness has reached the writer. Wanger (25) gives the content, methods, and some of the personal outcomes of an established unit on the Negro and his problems in a South Philadelphia high school for girls. This appears to have had striking results in overcoming prejudice, though no exact measurement has apparently been attempted. A group of forty girls shown by a pre-test to possess many prejudices and of whom only one or two "already had a fair point of view" were stirred to "amazement" and "enthusiasm" for Negro achievement by their reading. The change in attitude was developed further by visits of Negro speakers, chosen "not merely for the value of their message, but also for the interesting personalities." Teas to which the Negro speaker and Negro fellow students were invited by the class, and student programs of Negro accomplishment, were other influences. Evidence of change of attitude was found in student written testimony and projects.

The unpublished experiment by Schlorff already mentioned (22) appears to stand alone in its thorough and scientific procedure. Schlorff first constructed a social distance scale against which the racial attitudes of school children could be measured. This involved: (1) the selection of a set of personal relationships drawn from the everyday life of the child; (2) a random selection of the population from among students of the high school in which the experiment was to be conducted; (3) submission of the relationships to the subjects composing the population for paired comparison; (4) construction of a table of proportions of judgment; and (5) conversion of this table into a scale of sigma units by the formula used by Thurstone in his article "A Law of Comparative Judgment" (23). The preliminary list of nineteen personal relationships was then reduced to ten in such a way as to produce as nearly equal steps on the scale as possible. This elaborate procedure was adopted to meet three criticisms directed against the familiar list used by Bogardus: (1) that the scale is not experimentally determined, but assumed to coincide with reality; (2) that too few situations are used to serve as a really discriminatory scale of measurement; and (3) that situations are ranked rather than scaled, there being no evidence to show whether equal or unequal social distances exist between successive situations. Use of the scale in the rating of 20 nationalities by 425 high school students revealed the fact that the Negro stood lowest among those nationalities with whom the students had first-hand contact.

Schlorff then conducted an experiment to modify the attitudes of an experimental group of students in the direction of greater tolerance toward the Negro. The following steps were taken. (1) Two 9B civics classes were selected as experimental and control groups. (2) The fact was established that they were comparable as to factors which might affect the results, such as age, national background, mental ability, and emotional stability. (3) A list of twenty races and nationalities was submitted to both groups to be rated against the scale. (4) The experimental class was then exposed to a modified curriculum designed to increase its tolerance toward the Negro. The modified curriculum devoted 15 out of 36 forty-five minute Civics periods in one semester to the presentation of material concerning the Negro. This material included a knowledge of the Negro's origin, history, problem of adjustment to American life, and contribution to American culture, as well as discussion of the origins of prejudice toward and conflict with the Negro. These periods came at weekly intervals, alternating with meetings dealing with various other topics of the Civics course. In appearance they grew out of discussion on a chapter in the textbook headed "America—The Melting Pot" and general comments on the results of the race attitudes test. An excellent detailed description of the material content and the educational methods employed, together with the full bibliography used by the students, is given in Schlorff's unpublished dissertation (22:34-38, 40-41).

The fifth step was a re-rating by both the experimental and the control classes of the list of twenty races and nationalities against the scale to measure the influence of the curriculum. The experimental group now rated the Negro 1.23 units higher on the scale, the control group only .08. The deviation from the mean for this relationship was 1.09, or more than three times the standard deviation for the group of twenty relationships, which was .305, hence statistically significant (22:39). The relative position of the Negro remained the same in the case of the control group but in the experimental group it had risen above Portuguese, Greek, Russian, and Hungarian to rank 9, indicating on the scale acceptability as neighbor and almost as employer. Presumably those results were due to the modified curriculum.

Less discussion need be given to researches less closely related to the present problem. In the main they contribute findings either (1) on factors correlated with other race attitudes or with liberalism, or (2) on the effects of certain educational procedures on these attitudes. Orata (18:156, Study No. 76) and Hunter (13) found some slight correlation between age and tolerance, and Harper (10:320) between age and liberalism. Sex differences in race attitudes were slight in the studies of Bogardus (17:631) and Orata, and in liberalism according to Symonds (10:320, 1); Harper (10:320) and Harris and his associates (10:334) found women slightly less liberal than men. Several correlations found by Harris suggested to him "a tendency for women to be governed by parental and public opinion to a much greater extent than are the men. This tendency is not manifested much in their ideas, since they are only slightly less

liberal than men; but it is shown in their lack of outward mani-
festation of liberalism." (10:335) Little correlation was found
by Symonds between liberalism and amount of education of
the ordinary type, while Harper found a correlation of .5 in the
case of a larger and older population. Symonds found a correlation of .28 between liberalism and intelligence (10:323),
Harris .29 (149 men) and .09 (139 women). Harris concludes
that "other factors than intelligence are of most importance in
determining a person's liberalism or conservatism." (10:323)
Pintner found a correlation of .33 between neurotic tendencies
and generalized prejudice (using Watson's Test of Fairmindedness), but with attitude toward the Negro (using the Thurstone scale, Form A) only .11, and with other specific attitudes
still less (20).

On the other hand, Busch (4) and Lasker (14) emphasize
the expected close relationship between the attitudes of parents
and children, and Busch tentatively notes a geographical factor
in marked and unexpected antagonism toward people of other
races found in his replies from sections of the Middle West.
He found greatest race tolerance in New England and the
Middle Atlantic states, New York City, and Chicago (4:279).

Wheeler and Jordan (18:148, 9, Study No. 69) in a study of
the tendency of individual opinion to accord with group opinion found (1) that group opinion facilitates individual opinion
to an extent almost three times chance, while (2) group opinion
inhibits disagreeing opinion to almost one-half chance. Their
findings raise the important question as to the particular "group
opinion" used, for Watson's survey on American attitudes toward Orientals discovered social and economic class to play a
larger role than geographic location (26:231). Acquaintance
with individuals of different national groups has a striking influence on the rating given the groups themselves, according to
a study of national prejudices by Diggins (18:159, Study No.
79). On a scale of 10, in which the smaller number indicates

higher regard, the average position of all groups in which individuals had no intimate acquaintance was 6.14, one acquaintance 5.07, two acquaintances 4.50, three acquaintances 3.19, four acquaintances 2.65. The progression was equally clear among foreign students, International House Americans, and certain college groups. On the other hand, an educational tour of Japan by California high school pupils affected their opinions very little, though the mean gain in information was nine times the standard deviation (18:145, Study No. 65).

That racial attitudes can, however, be deliberately changed by even so brief an experience as exposure to a motion picture, is the evidence given by Thurstone from an experiment with a pro-Chinese and an anti-Chinese film. Using as a measuring instrument a scale constructed according to Thurstone's well-known methods, 182 children in Geneva, Illinois, were found to have a mean attitude score of 6.63 before, and 5.45 after, exposure to the pro-Chinese film. (High scores on this scale represent prejudice.) The ratio of the difference to the probable error of the difference was 16.98, representing a highly reliable change. The 172 children of West Chicago exposed to an anti-Chinese film showed less striking change, their mean attitude score before the film being 5.66, and after, 5.81, ratio of the difference to the P.E. of the difference 2.22 (24). Similar experiments with a variety of attitudes have been carried out by Thurstone, using motion pictures as the experimental factor. Permanence of these effects has been tested by repeating the schedules of comparison in several towns after an interval of four to five months. Speaking in general, Thurstone says: "The attitudes have returned about half way toward their original values in four months, but these effects vary of course with the film used and the frequency of other social stimuli. In one town the effect lasted without diminution for five months." What attitudes are meant was not indicated in the statement, but can be found in the report on all these experiments in published form (19). It appears that 117 of the pupils in Geneva, Illinois, exposed to the pro-Chinese film, held 62 percent of their gains after 5 months, and 76 held 60 percent of their gains after 19 months, as expressed by the ratio of the difference between the initial and the third mean and the difference between the initial and the second mean (19:53-5). The greatest change in attitude effected in any of the experiments with motion pictures was achieved with a powerfully anti-Negro sound-film to which 434 students from the sixth to the twelfth grade were exposed in Crystal Lake, Illinois. Very few or none had ever seen Negroes. The mean on the pre-test was 7.41, on the next test 5.93, and the difference divided by the probable error of the difference was 25.5. In a test five months later the means was 6.51, and the difference between the means of Test I and Test III, divided by the probable error of the difference, was 15.59. Sixty-two percent of this striking increase in hostile attitude was still apparent five months after the exposure to the anti-Negro film, showing a powerful and relatively permanent influence of the film in increasing prejudice against the Negro (19:35-38, 60-1).

Finally two important studies by Harper and by Biddle, measure the effectiveness of certain specialized and deliberate educational procedures. In connection with his larger research on the social beliefs and attitudes of American educators Harper (9) studied the influence in the direction of liberalism of certain courses in education "pursuing a type of thought-provoking study and discussion." His findings were impressive. At the beginning of a particular class the median liberalism-conservatism score of 196 educators was 53.6 (50 being the median score established by graduate educators of country-wide distribution, and 10 the standard deviation). At the close of the year after two to eight semester hours according to the election of the individual, the median score on the re-test was 68, a gain of 14.4. Among other groups and aggregates tested 193 individuals had

completed one or more courses of this particular type. To quote
from Harper:

> In no case did one of these classes make a median score below
> 65, which is 15 score intervals or 1.5 S.D. on the scale above the
> median score established by graduate educators of country-wide dis-
> tribution. On the other hand, a general aggregate of 755 educators,
> representative of the part of the student body not enrolled in these
> particular courses, made a median score of 53, a score only 3 inter-
> vals higher than the median score of graduate educators generally,
> and .6 lower than the median score made at the *beginning* of the
> year by the class whose remarkable gain during the year we have
> noted. No general aggregate of the student body, regardless of edu-
> cation level attained, was found to make a median score above the
> median score made *at the beginning of the year* by the class whose
> retesting *at the close of the year* established their median score at 68.
> It would seem difficult to escape from the conclusion that this un-
> usual score, representing a gain in median score of 14.4 intervals
> during the year, was due to the influence of the courses . . . taken
> (9:70-72).

Two more points should be observed. The larger study disclosed that extensions of the usual type of undergraduate education brought increases of a little less than two intervals per
year in median scores, and of the usual type of graduate education approximately four (9:75). In the case of 53 members
belonging to the specially influential course mentioned above,
cases whose signed tests enabled them to be studied individually,
the lower the score made at the beginning of the year the higher
the gain in score made during the year. Harper concludes:

> While the 53 members of the division as a whole made a gain of
> 15.3 in median score those of the division whose score made at the
> beginning of the year fell below the average for graduate educators
> showed a gain of 20.5 in median score, a rise of 2.1 S.D. on the scale
> during the year. For the 53 members of this division of the class, the
> correlation between original score and gain in score gave a negative
> coefficient of .849 ± .024. . . . The only way we can explain the
> lower original score made by these educators who showed such re-
> markable gains in scores during the year is to attribute these lower
> original standings to *the lack of appropriate stimuli in previous
> experience.* (9:72-73) (My emphasis).

Biddle attacked the problem of gullibility to nationalist propaganda by an experiment to increase recognition of and skepticism toward propaganda techniques (3). The experimental material consisted of nine specially prepared lessons entitled "Manipulating the Public." These were used in five high school classes and one college class. The period within which the nine lessons were covered varied with the different groups within the narrow limits of from one week to twenty days. A control group matched each experimental group in each institution, and to all twelve groups tests of "gullibility" were given before and after the lesson series. The test asked the student to rate on a graphic rating scale a wide variety of excerpts from articles on Pacific Relations, rating (1) the degree of fairness, and (2) the degree of truth or fact. The scoring key was made up by choosing the mode of twenty-four experts' markings on the graphic rating scale. Deviations were reckoned as positive or negative according to whether the subject was more sympathetic with the nationalist, or with the internationalist, sentiment of the excerpt than were the judges. While the test dealt with Pacific Relations, the illustrations given in the lessons were in other fields. Results of the test showed a difference in gains (i.e., reduction of score) between experimental and control groups that was highly significant and especially noteworthy in view of the relative brevity of the experimental period (3:50). Moreover, analysis of gains in certain control groups points to the unusual character of teaching done in the particular institutions.

It is worth noticing for the present experiment that Biddle suggests what he considers a more positive way of attacking the problem of propaganda than by the negative method of promoting skepticism. "For positive social thinking . . . new experience is needed . . . experience of a great variety of points of view in all controversial questions . . . an experience that is friendly and informative" (3:70).

Taken with the experiment of Schlorff, the results found by Harper and Biddle encourage confidence that a serious search for effective educational procedure to promote desirable social attitudes can be rewarded.

The last studies to be mentioned here concern measuring instruments used in the present experiment. The first of these was the scale of Attitude Toward the Negro developed by Hinckley, using Thurstone's methods (12). The Thurstone methods on various scales have been shown to yield a satisfactory reliability, and in terms of correlations between scores and case histories as evaluated by judges, a satisfactory validity (15:5).

In an article which makes accessible the core of his unpublished dissertation Hinckley (11) gives a detailed account of the development of the Negro scale, and answers the question whether the scale values are independent of the judges' attitudes. In the sorting of 114 carefully selected statements on the Negro he used three groups of judges totaling 850 (600 white and 250 Negro), from seven different states extending as far north as Pennsylvania and Maryland. The three groups differed definitely in their opinions as to the proper social position of the Negro. Group 1 was composed of students who just prior to the sorting checked the following two out of six proffered statements as expressing their own attitude toward the Negro: "Inherited qualities have predestined the Negro to the servant class of society," "The Negro should be used to produce the white man's needs" (11:288). Group II was composed of those who checked the following: "The white and colored races should enjoy the same privileges and protection as set forth by law," "Our refusal to accept the Negro is not based on any fact in nature, but rather on prejudice and should be overcome." (11:286-7) Group III was made up of the Negro students. (Students checking the pair of neutral statements and other combinations were not used.)

Three separate sets of scale values were calculated from the sortings of the three groups according to Thurstone's methods and the three groups carefully compared. In comparing the scale values of Groups I and II, $r = 0.980$. In comparing the scale values of Groups I and III, $r = 0.985$. The high correlations between the scale values obtained for the different groups indicated that the items selected for the final scale might about as well be selected from any one group as from any other. Actually the 32 statements chosen for the final scale were selected from the data of Group I, but since Group II placed them in the same rank order with one exception, "this is," as Hinckley says, "very definite evidence in favor of the objective validity of the scale" (11:293). On the basis of this and other supporting evidence Hinckley argues that, at least in countries where the social position of the Negro is an issue, the scale is not influenced in its measuring function by the attitudes of the subjects used in its construction (11:294).

Another scale of attitude toward the Negro utilized in the present experiment receives discussion in a recent study by Likert (15). This scale is part of a battery constructed by Murphy and Likert in connection with an investigation of international, interracial, and economic attitudes in various colleges. Likert's principal theme is a closely reasoned argument for measuring attitudes by methods of scoring simpler than those of Thurstone. First he found that a method employing sigma units correlated highly with results from the Thurstone methods, and at the same time avoided the necessity of raters and rating errors, permitted less laborious methods of constructing attitude scales, and yielded the same reliability with fewer items. A still simpler five-point method of scoring gave a correlation with the sigma method of .99 and with the Thurstone method of .83 or (corrected for attenuation) .92, and was therefore adopted (15:42, 3).

Incidentally to the main argument Likert reported other pertinent findings: (1) particulars on the qualities of the Negro scale as a measuring instrument, which will be given in discussing the present test battery (15:59, 60); and (2) evidence that clear-cut generalized attitudes toward the Negro as well as toward internationalism and imperialism exist. Likert began his investigation anticipating high specificity of attitudes. He expected, for example, that "attitudes toward segregation, toward eating with the Negro, and toward lynching would be independent, and that in general any one specific attitude toward the Negro would bear no clear relation to the attitudes on other issues" (15:11). He found on the contrary a clear-cut pro-Negro or anti-Negro sentiment. Though the stimulus situations of various items often appeared on the surface quite different, an emotional disposition ran through the entire list (15:38). "It is precisely in the field of *affiliation with* or *against* certain social groups," he says, "that the most definite results are obtained" (15:13). The bearing of this is of course that if attitudes are not purely specific, education is not limited to the laborious reconditioning of attitudes one by one, but may possibly alter many simultaneously through the general factor.

Likert emphasized the social or cultural character of the determining forces involved. "From the social-science point of view," he says, "it is valuable to recognize that these group factors are aspects of the cultural patterns shared by the . . . individuals . . . tested" (15:38). Distinct cultural areas could be defined quantitatively by a study of the similarity of test results, and in spite of large variations within each college group, sharply contrasting general trends were found to exist. "The relative number and strength of favorable forces is vastly greater at some colleges than at others" (15:40). A correlation of .40 between the scales of pro-Negro attitudes and internationalism, and of .34 between those of pro-Negro attitudes and imperialism, were held to point also to cultural causes rather than innate differences, though the possibility of a general radicalism-conservatism factor was mentioned.

III: Problem and Procedure of the Present Experiment

THE survey of previous research has disclosed at least one exact scientific experiment to modify attitudes toward the Negro through educational procedures and to measure the results. Like Hunter and Biddle, Schlorff employed thought-provoking academic materials of study in a scholastic setting to produce the desired shift in attitudes, and found measurable evidence of significant change.

The present experiment moves in a somewhat different realm just outside the recognized curriculum. It proposes to reduce social distance toward the Negro through organized intellectual and social contacts with representative Negroes and their community. Through the generous co-operation of many Negro leaders and groups a four-day "seminar" occupying two consecutive week-ends was set up, which provided orientation in the community, occasions of social hospitality, introduction to certain Negro accomplishments, and a variety of Negro views on American race relations. Such a procedure, like the others mentioned above, possesses the characteristic Watson recommends as most fruitful for attitude study, namely, experimentation to produce a change, but in addition it approximates what Bain has pointed out as the essential next step—duplication of life situations and the production of actual adjustment behavior (2:367). Bain adds the desirability of correlating verbal and overt behavior. This could ideally be carried to almost any lengths of observation and measurement of individual behavior, correlating these with specific statements of attitude. Such exact observation of individual adjustment behavior was quite beyond the resources of a pioneering study such as this, but a certain degree of correlation was found possible between the more obvious adjustments inevitable in the social contacts provided and certain responses on attitude tests. Clearly, an experiment of this sort calls for specific adjustments of habitual behavior, muscular and visceral as well as cortical, or (shall we say) physical and emotional as well as ideological, of a more direct kind than the adjustments to purely academic material. Though these cannot be charted by the present study, some idea of them can be gained by a description of the experience-series in Harlem which will be given with a certain degree of fullness further on.

Outline of the Experiment

In brief the stages of the experiment were as follows:

1. Administration of a test of attitudes toward the Negro to 354 students in six classes at Teachers College, Columbia University.

2. Selection of an experimental group of 46 from these classes in ways not obviously related to the testing program.

3. Exposure of the experimental group to a four-day seminar in Negro Harlem.

4. Establishment of a control group, equated by individual pairing of experimental and control group cases, on the basis of initial test scores.

5. Re-testing of the six classes, including the experimental and control group cases, again without obvious association with the Harlem experiences, approximately ten days after the seminar ended.

6. A voluntary social tea at the University, at which Harlem hosts and speakers were guests.

7. Individual interviews with members of the experimental group two months or more after the re-test to judge the effects of the seminar and to secure biographical and psychological details on the individual's race attitudes.

8. Ten months or more after the re-test a final re-testing (by mail) of both the experimental and the control group to measure permanence of the changes produced by the experimental procedure. With the test was enclosed a request for information on any pertinent influences experienced in the interval, and an estimate of experiences in New York.

The setting and procedure of the experiment need now to be described in greater detail.

The Setting of the Experiment

The immediate environment of the students with whom this experiment has to do is an immense graduate school of education in New York City. At the time in question it had 2,170 full-time and 3,212 part-time students, coming from many parts of the nation and from many foreign countries. Among them were a certain number of Negro students. As might be expected, attitudes toward the Negro among such a large group of students, faculty, and administrative staff cover a wide range from distinctly liberal to distinctly conservative. From time to time issues in classroom, dormitory, or social program bring the range of attitudes to focus, but in general opinion is diffuse, and objective conditions promote a certain kind of indifference to race, at least so far as educational activities are concerned. A Negro Education Club exists, and an annual series of lectures on problems of Negro Education has become an established tradition. The "thought-provoking courses" which Harper found so effective (9:69) in promoting liberalism form part of the setting. It is possibly true to say that liberalism is the better organized, but conservatism the more solidly entrenched in habit and custom, so far as these attitudes affect the Negro. Some members of the student body are connected with International House, whose activities promote acquaintance and appreciation of the cultures of many different races. Others study at Union Theological Seminary, where interracial activities are frequent. The general environment provides many stimuli to liberal opinion. On the other hand, large numbers of students coming from other environments are in attendance for one year only, and many do not venture far from their educational routine.

Neither faculty nor student body as a whole was at the time of the experiment actively conscious of the fact that at its doors is the largest Negro city in the world, though this has changed greatly in recent years. This lack of consciousness was due partly to the general North-to-South movement of traffic on Manhattan Island, partly to a line of cliffs which divides the university center on Morningside Heights from Harlem on the east, partly to the quiet but accelerating speed with which since 1910 the population of Negro Harlem has been arriving. The census for 1930 reports 224,670 Negroes on Manhattan Island out of 337,706 in New York City. Of these the great majority live in Harlem. Taken with the fact that the census tends to undercount as Negroes those who find it possible and desirable to "pass" as white, probably 200,000 Negroes live in the compact urban territory immediately adjoining Columbia University on the east and northeast.

In this community many of the leaders of Negro cultural life—in the fields of music, drama, literature, scholarship, religion, social research, public opinion, etc.—live or work. Broad avenues, well-built churches, certain fine streets, houses of moderate height present the outward aspect of a roomy residential district, while on the extreme east are well-marked slums. One of the best examples of recent urban housing architecture in this country is the Paul Lawrence Dunbar Apartments, with their park-like interior courts. An adequate characterization of this extraordinarily complex Negro city (roughly one-third Northern, one-third Southern, and one-third foreign-born from the British and Latin West Indies, South America, and Africa) would take us far afield.

The dramatic juxtaposition of these two contrasting environments did not alone facilitate arrangements for the seminar. Coe (6) in a pregnant analysis of the dynamic curriculum has outlined its content as follows: (1) explicit problems already felt by the learner, (2) implicit problems present in the situation but not yet felt, (3) problem-raising experience which extends the horizon for both learner and teacher, and (4) experiences involving mutual enjoyment without necessary connection with any problem. Under all four heads Harlem as neighbor is potentially rich in content for education, but for the university community as a whole this combination of geographical proximity and social distance presents an implicit problem of broad social importance. Whether for weal or woe this sphere of community interaction merits serious study.

The Test Battery and Scoring Methods

At bottom, proper evaluation of the outcomes of an experiment of this kind is dependent upon the availability of comprehensive and accurate techniques for its analysis, in short upon reliable and valid measuring instruments. With this condition in mind a composite test, made up of the best tests developed to date and supplemented by additional measuring devices created for the specific purpose, was determined upon as the measuring instrument for the experiment. Two parts of the battery were immediately available in, first, the Thurstone-Hinckley scales, Form A and B, "Attitude Toward the Negro" (12), and, second, items concerning the Negro contained in "A Survey of Opinions" constructed by Murphy and Likert (15), permission to use which was generously granted. Another section of the battery was made up of miscellaneous statements drawn from various sources. As no available tests were found which measured degree of acceptability of a Negro in any considerable variety of personal relationships, a social distance test was constructed which discriminated some fifty personal relationships, and registered degree of acceptability on a five-point scale. The social distance test was denoted as Part I, the Thurstone-Hinckley scales as Part II A and B, the Murphy-Likert items as Part III, and the miscellaneous items as Part IV. (See Appendix I, p. 129.) Two statements of relationship in Part I proved ambiguous, and were discarded in scoring (Nos. 38 and 39). Part II was scored in accordance with the Hinckley key for scale values, development of which is described in detail in his unpublished dissertation (11), and more briefly in a recent article (11). Likert has subsequently given evidence (15) in favor of a simpler method of 5-point or 3-point scoring in connection with the similar Thurstone-Droba scale "Attitude Toward War," but since this method not only was not at the time buttressed by his evidence, but also would have required some reconstruction of the directions and columns for responses in the printed Hinckley forms, it was not used. However, a simple method using integer score values between 1 and 5 was followed with the Murphy-Likert items, and throughout the rest of the test. It should be noted that Question 7 of the fifteen used by Likert in his "Survey of Opinions" was omitted in this battery as presumably a poor selector in a Northern graduate school of education. It measured the range of educational privileges to which, in the opinion of the subject, a Negro should be admitted. Likert gives statistical evidence to show that even with his widely distributed undergraduate groups it was a poor selector, in fact the lowest in his list (15:50, Table X). Finally it must be said that a few questions in Part IV which were cast in the form of statements of fact, though intended to test attitudes, were somewhat unsatisfactory.

Taken as a whole, this battery not only permits registry of changes of attitude by the experimental group, but provides data for a tabulation of attitudes toward a variety of issues as held by several hundred graduate students.

Soon after the beginning of the spring semester of 1932,

through the co-operation of four professors, the composite test was given to three classes in educational statistics, and to one each in international education, educational psychology, and methods of teaching. The test was administered either by the professors of these courses or by experienced testers introduced to the class for the purpose, but wholly unrelated to the later experiment. All followed the same set of directions, which made it clear that the test would not affect the student's grade or standing in any way, nor would individual test scores come to the professor of the course except in unidentifiable statistical form. The tests were signed, but the point was not labored in the directions. Students are accustomed to a great variety of questionnaires and tests at Teachers College, and no difficulty was experienced in their administration.

As most or all of these classes contained one or more Negro students, it was necessary to devise a plan for equal treatment during the test. This need was met by asking Negro students to fill out copies of a test by Dr. Charles Johnson of Fisk University, recording Negro attitudes toward white people, which he kindly provided. Furthermore, most of the Negro students were interviewed some time before the test was administered in order that they might understand its purpose and be willing to co-operate. The use of the Hinckley scales presented a delicate problem because both forms included expressions of extreme prejudice which might come as a tremendous emotional shock to Negroes who had been shielded from them. Hinckley himself reports an emotional explosion from this cause in a Negro college class which was asked to assist in the sorting process upon which the final scale was based (12:290). Consensus of advice from Negro students finally led to the use of these scales with white students, with safeguards intended to prevent their reaching Negro students without adequate forewarning.

As a result of the testing program 399 tests were received, of which 45 were eliminated either as unfinished, 7; defective, 3;

anonymous or under assumed name, 14; from foreign students, 9; or from Negro students, 12. Three or four tests of Canadian students were not readily discovered by inspection and are included. The net number of tests equaled 354.

Securing the Experimental Group

The experimental group was secured by invitation through the mail. No connection was made with the tests, and it is the testimony of the interviews that some students at least saw no connection between the testing program and the Harlem program until well after the re-tests were over, others until the re-test was given, and it appears that the great majority were not immediately conscious during the Harlem experiences that they were part of an experiment. In general, any connection between the testing and the Harlem seminar was drawn by the individuals themselves. No doubt this was done in some cases.

The mailing list was made up from the signatures on the signed tests. Addresses where lacking were supplied from the university directory. No invitations were sent to residents of International House because they were peculiarly liable to exposure to pro-Negro influences that might bias the experiment. For similar reasons Union Seminary residents (few in number) were omitted. Finally, invitations were not sent to out-of-town commuters because of the need to hold the experimental group together during two week-ends, including evenings. It was believed that as transportation difficulties began to be faced, some commuters who had underestimated them at the start might drop out of crucial experiences.

The text of the invitation is given in the Appendix. It will be seen that in getting a group on a voluntary basis for two week-ends the appeal rested primarily on unusual educational experiences and contacts with unusual people, open to a limited student group, by invitation, at negligible cost. Replies by enclosed post card expressing an interest in joining the seminar were received from slightly over eighty people. At the organization meetings the time-table and procedure of the seminar were given in detail, and it was announced that as numbers were limited, preference would be given to those planning to attend the full program. This method of fostering continuity of attendance worked surprisingly well, with only a few exceptions, due principally to illness or unforeseen professional or social obligations which intervened between the two week-ends. Appointment to membership in the group was confirmed by a reply post card, which gave instructions as to place and time of meeting and called for a reply stating, "I will join group for full program." In practice this was sent to all interested who had not previously indicated that the time-table was impossible for them. The final outcome was a membership of 46.

Those students interested in joining the seminar who yet in the end did not participate will receive attention subsequently. Obstacles of various kinds intervened between the expression of desire to join and the launching of the program, which ranged from inability to spare the required time, and pressure of work, to operations of *force majeure* such as summons out of town, conflict of program, illness, and even one accident a few moments after starting out. By study of the results from this group it will be possible to some extent to control the factor of volunteering in the experimental group.

The experimental group of 46 comprised those who actually entered on the seminar with the expressed purpose of taking it as a whole. The great majority did so, but a few, as was said above, attended only the first week-end, or its equivalent. It seemed legitimate to keep these few in the experimental group, first because their exposure to the stimuli had been both extensive and striking, and second, because their inclusion might be expected (if having any special effect) rather to penalize the experimental group than to aid it. They were therefore counted in in order to keep the group as large as possible.

The experimental group was found to be made up of 10 students from the South, 20 from the Middle West, 4 from the West, 11 from the East, and 1 from Canada. Ten were men and 36 were women. With scarcely an exception they were Protestant Nordics, mainly of Anglo-Saxon, but in a few cases of German, Scandinavian, or Dutch descent. There was one Jewish student. Later inspection also revealed that 21 out of 46 fell below the mean score attained on the total battery by the general student population of 354 tested.

The Harlem Seminar

Apart from the writer, who acted as the director and co-ordinator of the program, Negro men and women from various fields conducted all the activities of the seminar. To appreciate the psychological experience as a whole, some impression must be gained of various concrete aspects of it. In conceiving some of the emotional and habit adjustments involved it will be well to note attempts to smooth transitions, to graduate steps anticipated as new or difficult, to associate them with familiar stimuli, and to suggest their plausibility or inevitability by the nexus of the developing situation. Furthermore, familiarity with elements of the program will be needed to understand distinctions made by students in the subsequent interviews. One interesting finding from the interviews may be anticipated at this point: no item in the program failed to be considered among the three most valuable, and none failed to be considered among the three least valuable, of the experiences by one or more students, an evidence of the wide range of likes and dislikes in the group, though it must be added that the seminar was apprehended as a psychological whole to such a degree by most students that they usually objected in the interviews to conceiving the omission of any part. It should be emphasized that homogeneous rather than heterogeneous stimuli were deliberately selected from areas of real life hitherto little experienced, and arranged compactly.

The First Day. On assembling in a college classroom each member of the group was provided with a sketch diagram of Manhattan, a pamphlet of the Urban League possessing a map showing in black the extent of Negro Harlem, and a pamphlet survey entitled "The Negro Churches of Manhattan." These were not referred to again.

The group then walked ten blocks, half of which were familiar, to a residence club for Negro girls located in a block of brownstone houses, and took seats in its tastefully decorated social room. Here the editor of a nationally known Negro magazine interested in urban problems contributed perspective on Harlem from a number of points of view—the checkered history of the Negro in New York, uptown movements of Negro population, migration from the East South, real estate beginnings of Negro Harlem, its cosmopolitan population, the story of generations of Irish-Negro conflict in New York, and the sudden disappearance of antagonism about 1915 not due only to the cosmopolitan character of the city and to the tolerance arising from its strong minorities, especially the Jews, but particularly to the growing Democratic political organization of Negroes which suddenly resulted in Tammany protection. The result was a city in which Negroes are now relatively free from intolerance and antagonism, and in which the Negro does not want pity, but what he can get by being a citizen. As for the cabarets which often give Harlem its name, 90 percent of them are owned by shrewd white men for an outside public with Negroes for atmosphere. The speaker's witty and realistic analysis, together with his distinctly Negro appearance and color, were noticeable factors in the experience.

Following questions, the students were introduced in groups of three or four to Negro hosts as they arrived with their automobiles to show student guests the landmarks of Harlem. A fixed itinerary was followed, with personal explanations en route and stops by the whole group at various centers. In this way a general impression of the extent and character of the community was secured swiftly and comfortably, and some orientation achieved. Moreover, a host-guest relationship of limited extent had been experienced. Favored residential sections, such as "Sugar Hill" on a cliff overlooking much of the city, the blocks built by Stanford White, and the Dunbar Apartments already mentioned, leading churches, social centers, playgrounds, dance-halls, theaters, libraries, schools, and slum districts were reached by car and pointed out in transit. In particular stops were made and directors met at the Dunbar Apartments, St. Charles Borromeo Roman Catholic Church, directed by Irish clergy and with a partly white congregation, St. Mark's Methodist Church, a large modern Gothic church whose architecture had been ingeniously planned by a former Negro pastor to suit an unusual site, a lively playground and children's center under the direction of a recent Columbia graduate and athlete, and a ballroom representative of well-managed Negro recreation. The automobile survey ended at an attractive residence hall for girls managed by the Negro Young Women's Christian Association.

Dinner followed in a private dining room of the Y. W. C. A. For some this was their first experience in eating in a restaurant controlled by Negroes and a number were relieved that no colored people were to sit at their table. After dinner two addresses followed on Negro literature, the first an account of its past and present landmarks given by a distinguished woman novelist and poet of great personal charm and culture, who at the end consented to read poems of her own and others', the second an account of the development of Langston Hughes into a poet of social revolt skillfully illustrated stage by stage from his own poems, by a young woman friend of his. Here as elsewhere personal factors were at work in addition to the contents of the speeches; for example, the range and depth of personal culture of the one, and the radical protest of the other.

The last experiences of the day were by way of introduction to Negro learning and scholarship. Private access was granted after closing time to a near-by collection of rare books and manuscripts by and about the Negro covering three or four centuries. These were collected by a West Indian Negro scholar, and were maintained by the Carnegie Corporation. The collector gave an account of Negro contributions to cultural life in the American continents and Spain, illustrating it where possible with rare books in his own collection, and materials he found in the archives and libraries of Europe. An early treasure of the collection, for example, was an original edition (1573) of poems by a professor of Latin and Greek at the Royal College at Grenada, who had been an African-born slave, and became a protégé of Don Juan of Austria. This work was the earliest known individual contribution of a Negro to European culture. After the collector had opened up a number of fields of history through his books, his associate took the group through the shelf of new books by Negroes, characterizing them briefly. More lasting than what was said is probably the impression of the collector as a Negro scholar of wide and ripe learning, of Negro influence on history as pervasive, and of Negro creative writing today as of respectable volume.

The Second Day. The second day's experiences centered about religion and home life. As on the first day a meeting place at Columbia University was provided to permit going with a group if desired, and another simple approach into Harlem was taken by walking two blocks from the car line at City College down the City College hill to the Protestant or Catholic church selected. The Catholic service, which was attended by several members of the seminar, is notable for its setting of Gothic architecture and liturgical singing, and its interracial character with white clergy and Negro altar boys and white and Negro congregants.

The Protestant church, which the majority attended, is distinguished among Harlem churches for its thoughtful prophetic preaching, the fitness and dignity of its service, and its excellent music. In these qualities it is probably equal or superior to the churches most familiar to members of the seminar. It focuses interest in progressive social movements of the city and nation, and also co-operates with many local and national Negro activities. These characteristics stood out clearly in the session attended. A tradition of tactful welcome to strangers by members seated near-by was evident at the close.

Dinner, specially prepared and served for the group by a committee of women of the church, followed in the social hall. A number of Negro guests were invited as well, including the organist, one of the few Negro members of the American Guild of Organists, several of his soloists, and the young assistant minister, who gave a brief account of Negro church history in place of the pastor, who had been called out of town. The guests and the women's committee, most of whom were people of prominence in the community, were introduced to the group. A new influence that may be noted was acquaintance with an attractive young woman singer of Chinese and Negro parentage.

A visit was next made to an Episcopal church for a children's service, in which several hundred children are gradually habituated to Episcopal traditions of reverence and familiarity with Episcopal forms of worship. Particularly noticeable was their combined interest and order obtained without obvious restraint, and the stately Gothic interior of this prominent church.

At the close an impromptu talk given by the young rector to the group in the nave proved, according to the interviews, unusually impressive. After describing and illustrating the progressive educational principles on which his large Sunday School of 1,250, including 500 in the high school division, was operated and which he ascribed to his study with Coe, he explained his policy and outlook regarding race consciousness. Race consciousness he felt was bad and tended to separate people. His church was not race-conscious and avoided making young Negroes "Negro-conscious." "We don't want them off by themselves. We want them absorbed in all of American life." He expressed his disbelief in the existence of a unique Negro culture and Negro art in America, claiming that it was fundamentally American. He stated that many Negroes "pass" permanently into the white group annually, and that possibly in 250 years there would be no more black men in America. Doubtless some of his young people would eventually pass over, he said; on the other hand, it was conceivable that some of the student group before him had Negro blood without knowing it.

The final experience of the day's program was a social visit to the home of one or other of the two pastors met. The majority went with the rector to his home adjoining the church. There the family and a few friends, among whom some had acted as hosts with their automobiles the previous day, entertained the group, and the visit was used for acquaintance and social conversation which frequently turned on motives and activities of the students in the seminar.

A smaller group of twelve visited the other manse near-by, where the minister's wife (who had already been met during dinner at the church) entertained the group for tea. A number of young Negro musicians, a violinist, a soloist, and a pianist contributed a program of European music, and acquaintance was made with them, with some Negro university students, and with the children of the family. An atmosphere of hospitality was created, and later interviews showed that the hostess' casual description of difficulties she and other mothers met with in improving the school facilities for their children, as well as difficulties met in travel, was especially noted.

The second day obviously went beyond the first in providing experience of Negro groups as well as of individuals, and in calling for adjustments to decreased social distance in a number of new relationships. Some contact with the variety of Negro opinion on race relations had occurred, and, tacitly, striking evidence of the racially mixed character of the American Negro world had been gained by the inexperienced. This was particularly remarked in the choir of all colors at the morning church service. Appearance being so influential and so inevitably prior to acquaintance with personal qualities, these details are of some importance.

Interlude. A six-day interval elapsed before the next experiences. If the experiment had been of the laboratory type, it would undoubtedly have been ruinous not to have kept the subjects isolated under lock and key. Since, however, this experiment duplicates an educational procedure, the interlude was an undoubted asset. The stimuli to new intellectual, emotional, or habit reactions could be reflected upon, accepted or rejected, organized into one's experience in some form or other *in one's customary environment,* before new stimuli were received. That the environment might be hostile was discovered by some. One student was permanently "dropped" by two friends. Another was frightened out of continuing with the seminar. To sheltered individuals this discovery of the strength of racial feeling among fellow students was as educative regarding the nature of the American race problem as any addresses in the seminar. Moreover, ideas, viewpoints, and statements of fact were in many cases challenged rigorously. On the other hand, the possible bearing of opinion and custom on the lives of certain individual Negroes, now appreciated or admired, made issues more vivid.

The Third Day. No attempt was made to conduct members to Harlem personally on the third and fourth days. In general greater emotional maturity in social adjustments and in intellectual handling of controversial material was counted on and called for. More attention was given also to Negro disabilities.

The first event was a luncheon in the private dining room of a Negro restaurant, bringing together the Social Service Workers Club and the seminar. This club of Negro professional social workers represents many fields of community service, and expert knowledge of community needs—poverty, delinquency, health, housing, recreation, psychiatric social work, law enforcement, and other related social problems. Students and social workers were present in about equal numbers, and a good deal of interchange of ideas and interests took place at the various tables during lunch. After lunch current notices of the club, and a brief introduction by each one of himself and his work gave the entire party an idea of the activities represented. A speech on the question "Is Harlem Unique?" was then given by a research sociologist, resident and long-time student of Harlem, just then engaged in an extensive survey of a large neighboring city. In a series of paradoxes he brought out vividly the complexity of the peoples and social problems of Harlem, its extraordinarily varied groups and their interactions, the price in misery which it pays for congestion, the comparative freedom it enjoys, and its function as a provocative social laboratory. The account brought into relief a variety of handicaps faced by Negro communities, and answered the question as to Harlem uniqueness by "Yes and No."

Next came brief visits to various social institutions, including a large church with extensive social program and a public hospital conducted on interracial lines with white and Negro doctors, nurses, and patients.

Two addresses in the lecture room of a health center brought the afternoon to a close. A noted Negro surgeon, graduate of the Harvard Medical School, who had made specific contributions to medical science, discussed the health of Harlem and its relationship to poverty and discrimination. He reported that the only disease in which Harlem is unique in New York City is smallpox brought by the migration of Southern Negroes to the North. In addition he declared tuberculosis to be very prevalent, largely because of lack of money, resulting in improper food and living quarters, and lack of intelligence regarding proper care. Connected with this he mentioned a definite patent medicine menace. He discussed the suffering which has been inflicted on Negroes throughout the country by refusal of many hospitals to admit Negro patients, and the various obstacles which exist to bar Negroes from a medical education. He stated that the general tendency is to bar colored physicians from medical schools and hospitals. Bias was illustrated concretely in the policies of certain professional medical organizations. Nevertheless the correct solution was not, in the speaker's opinion, the policy favored currently by certain philanthropic foundations of building segregated schools and hospitals. The Negro physician can do his best work only when he is out among others, mixing, not as a colored person, but as another individual. Segregated institutions necessarily tend to inferior facilities and inferior professional standards. Describing the shift to an interracial basis of the hospital with which he is connected, and recounting its work, he showed how a segregation policy proposed in good faith by a certain foundation had been successfully discouraged in New York.

In connection with refusal of hospital attention to Negroes a current magazine was distributed to members of the seminar, giving an account of the tragic death of an internationally known woman dean after an automobile accident in the South. Many persons had expressed themselves as thinking that the accident need not have proved fatal apart from local hospital traditions against admitting Negroes.

A second address was given by the editor who opened the seminar a week earlier. One purpose in repeating a speaker was to bind together the two week-ends visibly, and to provide an unconscious gauge of gains in experience and outlook. This, together with social contacts enjoyed with other speakers and acquaintances of the first week-end at the luncheon, dinner, reception or Sunday tea of the second, gave to the peripatetic seminar values in a growing sense of familiarity and ripening acquaintance which inhere in a residential conference.

This speaker illustrated the striking contrasts in characteristics and in public opinion of various Negro communities, particularly Harlem and the Black Belt of Chicago. Like all other speakers of the afternoon he made it clear that the ultimate "hope, dream, aspiration and goal of every Negro in the United States" is complete participation in American life, but he showed how immediate objectives and tactics differ widely. In Chicago dominant opinion works toward a self-contained Negro community. Here in Harlem, on the contrary, race is subordinated; "the Negro does not consider himself a Negro, but a citizen of New York," his interest is the interest of a class, not of a race. With all poor people of New York his problems are—inadequate enforcement of housing rules, overcrowded school houses, municipal neglect of sanitation, lack of employment. A change is taking place in Negro life which so-called Negro leaders, too often chosen by whites, are unable to report or to represent, because they really know very little about what is going on, and are being increasingly disavowed.

Dinner was again held at the Y. W. C. A. The increasingly popular Negro "national anthem" by Rosamund Johnson was played and explained by the writer. What the social disabilities of the Negro in America mean in the growth of an individual was portrayed in an autobiographical speech by a young college woman who had experienced the differing environments of the Northwest, the deep South, and New York City. Like the surgeon and the editor, this former college student and teacher presented intimate discussion of the conditions which hurt and crush the growing personality, and the interviews showed that her veiled bitterness affected students in sharply contrasting ways.

The anticipated climax of the day was a party at a Harlem home which often serves as a rendezvous for writers and artists. Poised, sophisticated, well traveled, relatively free from color lines in their friendships and experiences, members of the Negro group kept dropping in with their friends until long after the seminar group had gone. After wraps were left in the private rooms, people returned to the reception rooms, decorated in Spanish Renaissance style, and sat on cushions on the floor informally for conversation, music, and eventually two witty talks by Rudolph Fisher and Nella Larsen, novelists. In the course of their remarks, which described the themes and special problems of the Negro writer, they teased each other, and twitted the group for its "slumming." When punch and cakes were served, people drifted throughout the house in conversational groups, and certain Southern girls and others of the group surprised themselves by assisting with the punch in the kitchen, and getting acquainted with a Siamese kitten in the hostess' room— to quote the interviews again.

The Fourth Day. Nothing was planned for the fourth day until tea-time. Actually a deluge of rain raged all day and together with a prevalent influenza reduced the white and Negro attendance at a tea given by the members of a sorority of college women. This was intended to bring together most of the speakers and hosts already met, as well as other representative people of Harlem not included on the program. After refreshments and a musical program, George Schuyler, editor, satirist, and member of a survey of Liberia, forecast the outlook for the future in sociological terms. On the basis of historical parallels and present developments he looked forward to a variety of expedients in racial adjustment, which would not, however, prevent the ultimate disappearance of the Negro in the general American population.

In the first draft of the seminar the program ended here, but practically all members who had not already heard Paul Robeson took advantage of an opportunity secured to go as a group to his final spring concert and to talk with him backstage. This was the only item in the seminar outside of Harlem, and in addition to the directly experienced enjoyment of a program of European and Negro music contributed the testimony of an enthusiastic white audience to Negro individual and folk talent. After the concert Robeson by request spoke of his experiences in the role of "Othello" in London, and discussed the possibility of overcoming difficulties in appearing in it here. In mentioning Negro folk songs he advised students to visit some of the more primitive church services in Harlem to hear them sung by the same type of folk as created them.

Summation. The nature of the experimental factor is now reasonably clear. It consisted in direct personal exposure to the complex influences exerted by middle-class Negro individuals and social groups—to their personalities, opinions, ideas, problems, worries, talents, achievements, and participation in community life. It created a psychological and social environment in which adjustments to progressively higher social forms of expression of the principle of democracy were stimulated and temporarily effected. Much is said of the educative value of travel. Part of this no doubt is due to the compulsory personal adjustments involved, which are not arbitrary in character, but which inhere in the process. As in the overcoming of physical distance which travel signifies, this experiment in overcoming social distance brought unmistakable realization of human variety within conventional groups, and according to many students' interviews produced awareness *for the first time* that many Negroes were indisputably superior in personal ability and character to themselves. Both in content and in method, then, this experiment occupies important but relatively neglected areas in education.

The Re-Test

The battery of tests was re-administered in the various classes, under as nearly identical circumstances as possible, eight to eleven days after exposure to the experimental factor ceased. No connection was made with the experiment, and the directions were the same, except for the opening remarks: "In connection with the investigation of students' race attitudes in which this class assisted on a previous occasion it is essential to ask students who filled out the questionnaire the first time to fill it out again. Do not try to recall how you answered the first time; simply answer as you feel at present." Because of absence or indifference (in one large class the test was given immediately before supper under completely voluntary conditions), 89 students failed to answer the re-test. Two hundred sixty-five cases remained, for which both test and re-test were available.

Securing the Control Group

The control group was secured by pairing each individual case in the experimental group with a corresponding case in the control group, pairing being done on the basis of initial scores on the attitude test battery. Taking the raw scores of the 265 cases on the first test, sigma scores were calculated for each part of the battery and for the battery as a whole, a mean of 500 and standard deviation of 100 being adopted to avoid negative numbers and to provide possibility of close comparison. All control group cases whose sigma scores on the total battery were within plus ten points or minus ten points of the total battery sigma score of a given case in the experimental group were temporarily grouped with that case. Plus and minus ten points meant that these different cases did not differ from the experimental group case by more than one tenth of a standard deviation in either direction. To locate the case in the control group having the best fit with the experimental group case on the separate parts of the battery, as well as on the total, the differences between their standard scores on each part of the battery were found, and the case for which the sum of the differences was a minimum selected. This was to insure as nearly comparable positions as possible in the different attitude surfaces measured by the separate tests and to avoid wide positive and negative discrepancies. Where cases were closely matched, sex or geographical factors were determinative.

The following illustration will demonstrate the procedure. First is given the sigma scores of a certain experimental group case and then two out of the sixteen cases which were tentatively grouped with it.

Matching by Sigma Scores

	Part I	Part IIA	Part IIB	Part III	Part IV	Total Battery	Divergence of Total Score	Sum of Divergence of Parts
Experimental	437	508	451	556	551	458		
Control 1	582	229	418	110	392	458	0	1062
Control 2	446	458	418	576	569	454	—4	130

Though the first control group case agrees exactly with the experimental group case in total score, the second is preferred because its agreement in the separate parts is much closer. With the first case it is evident that the apparent perfect agreement between the total scores is illusory and merely represents perfect balancing between positive and negative discrepancies in the various separate sub-tests.

Comparison of the Control and Experimental Groups

The control group which was secured by these means, and the experimental group show a reasonably close similarity in a number of factors. As evidence of the closeness of the pairing, the means of the two groups differ by only .02 of a standard deviation of the initial distribution. In terms of raw scores the mean of the experimental group is 364.85, and of the control group 364.78, the respective standard deviations being 56.13 and 56.81. The greatest difference in total *raw* score between members of a pair is 7 units. In terms of sex 36 of the experimental group are women, 10 are men, as compared with 31 women and 15 men in the control group. In terms of geographical environment during the first twenty years of life, in the experimental group 10 are from the South, 20 from the Middle West, 4 from the West, 11 from the East, and 1 is a Canadian citizen; in the control group 6 are from the South, 15 from the Middle West, 1 from the West, 22 from the East, and 2 are American citizens brought up in Canada. There seems to be little difference in national descent, the control group being apparently almost equally Nordic, with one or two more Jewish students and one student of Italian descent. The mean age of the experimental group is 33.6 years, of the control group 33.2. Intelligence scores could not be compared because of incomplete records. Further comparisons, which involve the experimental factor, will be made in the next chapter.

With the re-testing the experiment proper came to an end. Before discussing supplementary measures of the effects of the experiment an analysis of the findings of the more exact measuring instruments will be given.

IV: Analysis of the Test Results

THE purpose of the present experiment, it may be recalled, was to ascertain whether by the means described measurable results in increased favorable attitudes toward the Negro could be produced. It is time now to examine the results of the measurements to see how far, if at all, such evidence was obtained. The present chapter will report (1) the behavior of the test instruments, (2) the comparative standing on the attitudes test of the experimental group and the main group tested, (3) the general results apparently associated with the experiment, together with an examination of possible factors involved, and (4) evidence of shift in specific attitudes.

Reliability of the Measuring Instruments and
Intercorrelation of the Scores

Two of the four members of the test battery, as was indicated in Chapter II (pp. 22-24), have already been examined for their reliability and validity by Hinckley and Likert respectively, who prepared them in their own research. Hinckley's scale rests not only on the generally accepted validity and reliability of the Thurstone methods of scale construction, but also on his own demonstration that though prepared from the judgments of judges unfavorable to the Negro it measured equally well the attitudes of judges friendly to the Negro (12:292-4). Likert found reliability coefficients for his Negro scale by the split-half method, which ranged with eight groups of subjects from .65 to .83 for raw scores, and .79 to .91 when corrected for attenuation. Thirty-day re-tests gave in two cases coefficients of .72 for raw scores, and .85 when corrected (15:29). The fourteen items used were not the same in these calculations as they were in the test battery since Likert omitted the item regarding dis-approval of the term "nigger," and kept the item on degree of education to be granted Negroes, which was omitted in this battery as a poor selector (15:18). His argument for validity rests on general considerations brought out by previous research and on the statistically significant difference found between the mean score of the lowest of the Northern college groups he tested and that of a college group in Virginia. The difference in means when divided by the sigma of the difference was 8.3, a reliable difference.

In the present experiment the reliability of the several parts of the test battery and of the battery as a whole was obtained from the re-tests of 219 students not exposed to the experimental factor (265 less the experimental group), with an interval of five weeks between the tests. Table I presents the re-test reli-

TABLE I

RE-TEST RELIABILITY OF NEGRO ATTITUDE TEST BATTERY (N = 219)

Part	Title	Initial Mean	S.D.	Re-test Mean	S.D.	r
I	Smith	106.33	45.20	101.08	45.40	.89
II A	Hinckley A	72.71	10.30	72.73	9.90	.70
II B	Hinckley B	69.85	12.50	70.70	12.34	.68
III	Murphy-Likert	55.98	5.36	55.92	5.28	.83
IV	Miscellany	51.08	5.71	51.37	5.60	.81
	Total Battery	355.96	67.98	351.80	68.61	.92

ability coefficients for the parts and for the total battery, together with the means and standard deviations for the two administrations on which they were calculated. It will be observed that all the instruments have a fairly high reliability. The somewhat higher figure for the Smith test is no doubt partly associated with the pattern form of the test itself. On the other hand, the fact that the Thurstone-Hinckley scales are quite the lowest in reliability (Form A .70 and Form B .68) is somewhat surprising in view of their reputation and the careful way in which they were developed. In any case, a re-test reliability coefficient of .92 seems to indicate a very satisfactory reliability for the battery as a whole, and justifies its use as an index of shift in attitudes as a result of the experimental factor which was utilized.

The intercorrelations of the tests with each other and with the total are given in Table II, which is based on the initial scores

TABLE II

INTERCORRELATIONS OF TESTS OF ATTITUDE TOWARD THE NEGRO (N = 354)

Part		IIA	IIB	II Total	III	IV	Total *	Total ‡
I	Smith	.55	.61	.67	.68	.68	.96	.85
II A	Hinckley A		.52		.56	.56	.70	.77
II B	Hinckley B				.59	.67	.76	.82
II	Hinckley Total							
	I, III, IV combined	.76			.66	.71	.84	.87
III	Murphy-Likert					.70	.78	.85
IV	Miscellany						.79	.87

* When the scores are summed.
‡ When all the tests have equal weight in the total score.

of the entire 354 students tested. The correlations of the separate sub-tests with the total are all relatively high (.70 to .96), and sufficiently low with each other (.52 to .71) to indicate that the test gains in effectiveness by the inclusion of all five sections. The high correlation of the Smith test with the total (.96) is affected no doubt by its length and large numerical contribution to the total score. When by summing sigma scores for the separate parts of the battery a score is obtained in which all the tests have equal weight, all the other correlations rise somewhat, while the former declines. For this investigation, however, the Smith test, which in terms of acceptable social relationships with Negroes deals most closely with the experimental factor, is presumably not unduly weighted. The total score on the combined Hinckley scales showed a higher correlation with the total battery than did either scale taken alone. When all five scales were given equal weight in the total score, the correlation of Form A with the total was .77, of Form B .82, and of the combined Form A and B .87. Taken singly, the Hinckley scales showed the lowest correlations with the total score, regardless of which kind of total score was used. Moreover, definite differences between the two forms seem apparent, a fact which has its bearing on the practice of using the two forms separately or interchangeably. Form A of the Thurstone-Hinckley scales obtained a much lower correlation with Form B than one would expect for forms that are comparable (.52). Since these intercorrelations were taken under ideal conditions, that is, at the same time, this fact is striking. If used separately, Form B, which has a higher correlation with every other part of the battery and both forms of the total, seems preferable. Part III and Part IV, in view of their brevity (14 and 15 items respectively), correlate satisfactorily with the total. It seems clear, finally, that the battery as a whole gains by the inclusion of all its sections. In correlation with the sigma score total, which has the effect of eliminating the factor of difference in length, all the sections obtained reasonably high coefficients.

Comparative Attitude Levels of the Various Groups Toward the Negro

A base line against which to measure the various groups in their relative attitude toward the Negro at the start of the experiment is supplied in Table III. The left-hand section presents an analysis, in terms of raw scores, of the largest sample of Teachers College students tested, from which the smaller groups were drawn. High scores represent favorable attitudes toward the

TABLE III

INITIAL TEST RESULTS ON NEGRO ATTITUDE TEST BATTERY FOR TOTAL, PARTIAL, AND EXPERIMENTAL GROUPS

Part	Title of Test	354 STUDENTS TAKING FIRST TEST			265 STUDENTS WHO ALSO TOOK RE-TEST		46 STUDENTS EXPERIMENTAL GROUP	
		Mean	*S.D.*	*Range*	*Mean*	*S.D.*	*Mean*	*S.D.*
I	Smith Acceptable Relationship Test	104.16	45.03	8-198	106.97	44.04	109.00	40.62
II A	Thurstone-Hinckley Scale, Form A	72.97	10.47	32-100	73.22	10.05	75.63	8.44
II B	Thurstone-Hinckley Scale, Form B	70.07	12.62	37-100	70.10	12.36	71.30	11.53
III	Murphy-Likert Test Items on Negro	55.80	5.42	36-65*	56.11	5.15	56.72	3.96
IV	Miscellany	50.89	5.88	35-61*	51.10	5.68	51.20	5.62
	Total Battery	353.90	68.99	186-520	357.51	66.14	364.85	56.13

* Upper limit of possibility.

Negro. To improve the weighting of the different tests in the battery represented, the key values of the Thurstone-Hinckley scales have been multiplied by 10. No norms for these scales had been established, but the Form A mean of 72.97 may be compared with a mean of 75.47 calculated from data gathered by Pintner in a class of 53 mature students in mental testing. A clearer indication of the standing of the group in regard to attitude is obtained by a comparison with college groups tested by Likert (15:32). For nine student groups covered by his study, ranging in size from 32 to 123 cases, in Eastern, Midwestern, and Southern colleges, the group means on the fourteen Negro items used here ranged from 42.13, obtained by a Southern college group, to 55.21, obtained by a college group in New York City. The Teachers College sample of 354 cases, with its mean of 55.80 on these items, obtained a slightly more favorable mean score than the most liberal group in his study. Moreover, only 5 of the 354 cases, 4 of Southern and 1 of Massachusetts origin, fell below the mean of his lowest group. (These means were calculated by the writer directly from Likert's data sheets to remove the effect of his Question 7, omitted as a poor selector from this battery, and they therefore do not correspond with Likert's table.) If one should apply the printed interpretation of the Thurstone-Hinckley scale values to the scores on Form A, not a single case of "prejudice" would be detected, an indication not only of the relatively liberal standing of the group in question, but (more significantly) of the slight importance that *relative* liberality possesses in the present situation in view of the amount of social distance actually existing, as will be shown later. Other quite different definitions of "prejudice" are of course possible with the Thurstone-Hinckley scale (the acceptable relationship test of the battery possesses finer discriminating power in this respect), but it is nevertheless fair to say that as groups go, the group in question has a relatively high standing in respect to favorable attitudes toward the Negro.

The 89 students who failed to take the re-test were on the average slightly less favorable toward the Negro. This is apparent in the figures giving the means and standard deviations of the resulting group of 265. In every part of the battery there was a slight increase in mean score, and a slight decrease in standard deviations with the departure of the extreme cases.

A final comparison helps define the experimental group. It is in every part of the test slightly more favorable to the Negro in mean scores, and slightly more homogeneous, as disclosed by the standard deviations, than either of the other groups. In no case, however, are the transitions striking. The paired control group naturally shares the mean status of the experimental group. The experiment took place in a relatively liberal environment on a group of students slightly more liberal, on the average, than the total group of students tested.

Summary Evidence of the Results of the Experiment

In Table IV preliminary answers are given to the questions: Did measurable changes of attitude take place in the experimental group? What was the nature of these changes? Were they sufficiently different in amount from any simultaneous changes in the control group to be reasonably ascribable to the experimental factor itself rather than to other influences in the environment?

Table IV presents the standing both of the experimental and of the control group on the initial test and the re-test, and permits various interesting comparisons. First to be noted are the close approximations of the means of the two groups in all five parts of the initial test, as well as in the grand total. In no case does the difference amount to a whole unit. Such agreement is of course due to the particular method adopted for individually pairing the two groups, which was described in Chapter III. The standard deviations for the total and two of the parts also correspond closely, but differ most in the Thurstone scales. The

TABLE IV

INITIAL AND RE-TEST RESULTS ON ATTITUDE BATTERY FOR PAIRED CONTROL AND EXPERIMENTAL GROUPS (46 PAIRS)

Part	Title of Test	INITIAL				RE-TEST				RE-TEST CORRELATION	
		Control		Exper.		Control		Exper.		Control	Exper.
		Mean	S.D.	Mean	S.D.	Mean	S.D.	Mean	S.D.	r	r
I	Smith	109.83	40.31	109.00	40.62	105.52	41.78	130.17	38.80	.87	.82
II A	Hinckley A	75.28	6.66	75.63	8.44	75.56	7.50	81.39	9.26	.56	.48
II B	Hinckley B	70.70	10.14	71.30	11.53	71.63	10.81	82.39	11.07	.66	.42
III	Murphy-Likert	57.26	4.02	56.72	3.96	56.96	3.93	59.52	4.49	.76	.50
IV	Miscellany	51.72	4.61	51.20	5.62	52.44	4.82	55.26	4.87	.68	.78
	Total Battery	364.78	56.81	364.85	56.13	362.11	59.24	408.74	57.33	.88	.80

Thurstone scales also have the lowest re-test reliability coefficients. In the smaller group of 46 all the re-test reliability coefficients are lower than they are in the group of 219 students discussed, but nevertheless the re-test reliability coefficient of .88 for the grand total is sufficiently high. Comparing the initial and re-test means of the control group reveals slight gains in the miscellany and the two Thurstone scales, a slight loss on the Murphy test, and a larger loss on the Smith acceptable relationship test. This may have been due in part to a finer discrimination of position on the steps of the relations, to a more negative mood toward the test, to greater candor, or simply to accident. In general the standard deviations increased. The mean for the grand total slightly declined.

Comparison of the experimental group test and re-test means immediately reveals gains all along the line, amounting in the grand total to approximately 44 points. There is no general trend of any kind in the standard deviations, but in the social distance test the group becomes slightly more homogeneous in outlook. The coefficients of correlation between the initial test and re-test are of course not "reliability" coefficients. As might be expected, they are smaller than the reliability coefficients of the control group (except in the miscellany), since the shift to new positions in attitude would not be likely to take effect consistently. That gains in degree of favor expressed toward the Negro have occurred in the case of the experimental group and that these gains are independent of changes in the control group is evident from this table.

How statistically significant are these changes? What is the likelihood that these changes might have occurred by chance? Table V presents evidence that the gains are statistically significant. If a difference 3 or more times the standard error of the difference is accepted as the index of a true difference, then with one exception the differences appear to be quite highly reliable statistically. In fact, even in the case of the one test where the

TABLE V

Significance of Differences Between Re-test Means of Paired Experimental and Control Group Cases (First Re-test) (46 Pairs)

Part	Title of Test	$Mean_{Exp.} -$ $Mean_{Con.}$	$S.E._{Diff.}$ *	$\dfrac{Diff.}{S.E._{Diff.}}$
I	Smith Acceptable Relationship Test	24.65	4.83	5.10
II A	Thurstone-Hinckley Scale, Form A	5.83	1.37	4.25
II B	Thurstone-Hinckley Scale, Form B	10.76	1.76	6.11
III	Murphy-Likert Items on Negro	2.56	.89	2.89
IV	Miscellany	2.83	.74	3.79
	Total Battery	46.63	6.33	7.36

* The difference was obtained for each of the 46 pairs. The mean and S.D. of each of these 46 differences were computed and the S.E. of the mean was obtained by the usual procedure.

difference does not quite meet the above standard, the difference is so large that it would occur by chance only about 4 times in 1,000 samples. Differences in the acceptable relationship test, the Hinckley scale Form B, and the grand total, measured by quotients of 5.10, 6.11, and 7.36 respectively, are still more emphatic. So far as the outcome of the experiment can be reduced to brief symbolic expression, the crux of the experiment has been reached, and it has been ascertained that significant increases in favorable attitudes toward the Negro can be effected during a period of time as brief as two consecutive week-ends by such contacts as the Harlem Seminar provided, for students comparable to the Teachers College students who were exposed to this experiment.

Factors Possibly Involved in the Gain

What kinds of students are most likely to have a relatively favorable attitude toward the Negro? And what kinds of students are most likely to develop a favorable attitude as a result of cultural contacts of the kind described? In other words, what factors correlate highly, slightly, or negatively with high scores in the initial group, and what factors with gains during the experiment?

The relationships between age, intelligence, sex, and geographical region of upbringing, and scores on the initial test were first studied. As far as possible, the entire group of 354 students were used as representing the largest sample available before any special factors had been introduced. In order to equalize the weight of the various tests of the battery, and thus correlate the factors with favorable attitude as defined jointly by the five instruments, sigma scores were calculated for each part of the test, using 500 as the mean and 100 as the standard deviation, and the five separate scores summed, divided by 10 and rounded off, as in the basis for calculating the intercorrelations.

In this way the relationship was not complicated, as under the raw score method, by the fact that certain parts of the battery had larger variability than others.

Age. The correlation was calculated between chronological age in years and sigma scores for 354 students on the first test. The coefficient of correlation was .04. In other words, relationship between age and attitude score was practically nil. The evidence seemed to indicate the probability that favorable attitudes toward the Negro among adults neither increase nor decrease appreciably with age. The mean age was 33.09.

Intelligence. The correlation with intelligence was calculated for 159 students on the basis of scores available on the Teachers College General Examination, a thorough intelligence test of the usual college type. A somewhat more positive, but still slight relationship was found, the correlation being .13. Intelligence apparently is an almost negligible factor in the shaping of attitudes toward the Negro, very much as Symonds found to be true in the case of liberalism. Presumably accidental or group conditioning of emotions will eventually be found more significant.

Sex. Though age has been found of slight importance in differentiating scores, age differences between men and women among the 354 students may be given before studying their difference in score. For 119 men and 235 women, the men's mean age was 32.13 with S.D. of 7.31, the women's mean age 33.58 with S.D. of 7.89, the men being younger by a mean difference of about one year and a half (—1.45). A study of scores by sex seemed to reveal sex as a fairly important differentiating factor. The mean for the whole group in terms of sigma scores was 247.88 with S.D. of 43.00. For men alone the mean score was 256.44 with S.D. of 43.47; for women the mean score was 243.54 with S.D. of 42.10. The men's higher mean score of 12.90, divided by 4.84, the standard error of the difference, gives an index of 2.66. In other words, there are only about 8 chances in 1,000 that a difference as large as this would occur by chance in a random sample from a population in which the true difference was zero. This result is strikingly like the findings of Harris, Symonds, and Harper in various studies of liberalism, in which they found about 98 chances in 100 of a true difference between men and women (10:323). On the whole there was a tendency for men to be slightly more liberal than women in the specific field of attitude toward the Negro as well as in more general attitude areas.

Geographical Environment in Childhood and Youth. Another grouping was made according to the region in which the individual had spent most or all of the first twenty years of his life. Table VI indicates the classification and the relative standing of the various areas. A suspicion that Ohio, Indiana, and Illinois, which have received a large influx of Negro emigrants from the Central South in recent years, might show greater antagonism led to this group of states (referred to in the table as the Ohio group) being studied separately. New York State being of special local interest also received separate attention. No attempt was made to study the small number of nine students

TABLE VI

INITIAL TEST TOTALS BY GEOGRAPHICAL REGION OF EARLY RESIDENCE, BIRTH TO TWENTY YEARS (N = 354)

Region	N	Mean	S. D.	Rank Order
West	20	256.25	28.84	7
Ohio Group *	42	253.62	44.18	6
New York State	69	252.55	39.28	5
New England	42	250.43	41.96	4
Mid-West less Ohio Group	69	248.59	41.26	3
Middle Atlantic	49	244.96	43.92	2
South	54	233.65	48.12	1
Canada	9	——	——	

* Indicates Ohio, Indiana, and Illinois.

brought up in Canada. Contrary to expectation, the Ohio group of students had the most liberal standing of all the larger groups, second only to the small Western group. Whether this is in part due to the recent occurrence of the Negro migration, to the previous tradition of anti-slavery sentiment, or to the accidental factor of selection in the student group represented, to a class factor, or to an erroneous hypothesis to start with, may be conjectured. So far as it goes, this finding is somewhat at variance with the tentative conclusion of Busch (4:279). The South, as might be expected, has markedly the lowest mean score in terms of attitudes measured by this kind of test. The Middle Atlantic states occupy lowest place among Northern states, while New England has only average position.

None of these differences by geographical areas, however, are statistically significant. The variation among the means of these seven regions is not reliably great in relation to the variation within regions. Therefore it is reasonable to combine the regions and treat them as one homogeneous group, and no explanation of the differences need be sought.

The geographical factor is not unimportant, but as Watson's

investigation of opinion on Pacific relations has shown, it is not so important as is usually assumed (26:231). Moreover, even on race relations Southern opinion has not now, if it ever had, the solid front often ascribed to it.

It would have been interesting to correlate scores with other factors if they had been available. In order not to weigh down the extensive test, or distract attention from the test, geographical origin was the only biographical question asked directly in the questionnaire, data on age, and sex when not indicated by the name, being secured from the university records.

The Relation of Gains in Score and Certain Other Factors— Degree of Interest

In analyzing the marked gains evident in the case of the experimental group a matter of importance is the degree of weight to be given to the factor of interest. The experimental group was self-selected by virtue of individual response to a letter of invitation to join in the Harlem experiences, and represented those whose interest was sufficiently great that they agreed to devote two week-ends to the seminar opportunities. It may be argued that the gains are mainly ascribable to the factor of interest. Such a question cannot be completely answered. On the other hand, its importance must not be exaggerated. Interest is a factor implicit in the provision of elective courses and elective experiences generally in education, and by no means discredits the achievement of the educational agency. How practicable in education would it be to plan experiences such as the Harlem seminar for an indifferent group? None the less it is desirable to measure as far as possible the relative bearing of the experiences themselves and the readiness with which the students approached them. A certain indication, important as far as it goes, was the frank statement in an interview made by one student, who said that if interest had not kept climbing and climbing, she would certainly not have attended the second week-end. In other words, the experiences themselves created interest subsequently.

A more objective check is made possible by the considerable group of students who expressed a desire to join the seminar, and who in varying degrees exerted themselves in that direction. In certain cases no doubt a real difference in drive existed, which if brought to equality of intensity with the experimental group cases, would have overcome minor obstacles. In other cases the drive was positively known to be adequate, but circumstances of *force majeure,* including positive illness or unavoidable absence from the city, intervened. The clearest case is that of the person who went through the entire preliminary stages and started out with the group only to suffer a fall and sprained ankle at the outset.

After eliminating individuals who did not take the re-test, or whose tests were incomplete or defective, 23 cases remained, all of whom had indicated their desire to join the seminar, yet for one reason or another had been prevented. This group was called the "interested control group," and each case paired with a corresponding case, of approximately identical initial score, in the experimental group. One cannot say that the interest of these two groups was absolutely equivalent, in that one group actually went on the seminar and the other did not, but that the factor of interest was of sufficiently close comparability to make the results of these comparisons of peculiar concern is apparent. Table VII indicates the results of the comparisons and should be viewed with Table V.

Rather close pairing was effected between the two groups thus formed. For the new experimental group the initial mean score on the total battery was 349.83 with a standard deviation of 48.59, and for the control group 350.03 with a standard deviation of 48.14. In the re-test, however, the two groups diverged markedly. Sizable differences in means were evident between the experimental group and the "interested" control group on

TABLE VII

SIGNIFICANCE OF DIFFERENCES BETWEEN RE-TEST MEANS OF PAIRED EXPERIMENTAL
AND "INTERESTED CONTROL GROUP" CASES (23 PAIRS)

Part	Title of Test	$Mean_{Exp.} -$ $Mean_{Int.\,Con.}$	$S.\,E._{Diff.}$	$\dfrac{Diff.}{S.\,E._{Diff.}}$
I	Smith Acceptable Relationship Test	16.89	6.75	2.50
II A	Thurstone-Hinckley Scale, Form A	7.43	2.76	2.69
II B	Thurstone-Hinckley Scale, Form B	9.43	2.71	3.48
III	Murphy-Likert Items on Negro	2.87	.82	3.50
IV	Miscellany	3.57	1.23	2.90
	Total Battery	49.74	8.40	5.92

all parts of the battery and on the total, showing that definite gains in more favorable attitudes had been registered by the experimental group. The difference on the total battery and on three of the sub-tests was in fact quantitatively larger than the corresponding difference between the complete experimental and the original control group, and was nearly as large on the Thurstone-Hinckley scale Form B. This is particularly noteworthy because the new groups were only half as large. Moreover, though the differences, divided by their standard errors, produced indices in every case smaller than in the earlier comparison, this is due chiefly, of course, to the fact that the present comparisons were based on only 23 pairs rather than 46 pairs. On three of the five divisions of the battery the difference was not statistically reliable, as measured by the usual index of three. Evidently there is a bare possibility that the differences in gains on these three sub-tests might be wiped out in other samplings. But the fact that the total battery, Thurstone-Hinckley Scale Form B, and Murphy-Likert items all registered statistically significant gains with half the number of cases, while the other results approached 3 fairly closely, makes it fair to conclude that original interest and inclination had only a minor in-

TABLE VIII

CERTAIN POSSIBLE DIFFERENTIAL FACTORS IN EXPERIMENTAL GROUP GAINS

Factor	Number in Group and Description		Mean Gain		S.D. Gain		$Mean_A - Mean_B$	$S.E._{Diff.}$	$\dfrac{Diff.}{S.E._{Diff.}}$
	A	B	A	B	A	B			
Initial test score	23 (below mean)	23 (above mean)	51.70	36.09	33.91	35.41	15.61	10.4	1.50
Mean age	23 (below mean)	23 (above mean)	49.39	38.39	37.77	32.24	11.00	10.6	1.04
Sex	36 (women)	10 (men)	45.86	36.80	35.89	33.30	9.06	12.9	.70
Geography	11 (from East)	10 (from South)	53.00	38.80	30.37	29.24	14.20	13.7	1.04
Geography	11 (from East)	24 (from Middle West and West)	53.00	42.33	39.37	39.81	10.67	13.9	.77
Geography	24 (from Middle West and West)	10 (from South)	42.33	38.80	39.81	29.24	3.53	14.4	.24

fluence on the experimental gains, and that the nature of the experiences was the dominant factor in the increase in pro-Negro scores.

A series of other factors were studied for their possible bearing on gain in score in the experimental group but without finding any statistically significant. (For summary see Table VIII.*) Nevertheless they represent certain tendencies which are suggestive. As in Harper's study of the effect of certain thought-provoking courses on liberalism, cases below the mean gained more than those above the mean, thus tending to support the idea that low scores previously might be due to lack of appropriate stimuli. On the average, the younger subjects gained more than the older, the women more than the men. Is this also perhaps due to more restricted previous exposure to stimuli which promote favorable attitudes. toward the Negro? This theory *prima facie* hardly applies in relation to the geographical findings, unless one assumes that it is more than counterbalanced by contrary factors. The Eastern group of students gained more than the Middle-and-Far-Western group, and more than students from the South. The mean gain of Western students was not, however, much larger than that of Southerners. One of the most striking instances of gain was actually in the case of a student from the South.

Changes on Particular Items of the Tests

Finally, consideration needs to be given to shifts and changes on individual items of the tests. These will be analyzed first numerically and absolutely, and then comparatively in reference to the large group.

It was decided at the outset to study all marked pro-Negro

* The standard deviation of the difference of the means was computed according to the formula:

$$S.E._{Diff.} = \sqrt{\frac{N_1(S.D._1)^2 + N_2(S.D._2)^2}{N_1 + N_2 - 2}\left(\frac{1}{N_1} + \frac{1}{N_2}\right)}$$

TABLE IX A

VERY LARGE PRO-NEGRO SHIFTS MADE BY EXPERIMENTAL GROUP FROM INITIAL TEST TO RE-TEST, BY ITEMS (46 CASES)

Item No.	Item	Response on Which Shift Occurred	Percentage of Shift on Given Response	Most	Many	Some	Few	No	Yes	Uncertain	Approve
I 13	Traveler—same table	No	−20		+26*	− 2	− 4				
15	Same stateroom on boat	No	−39		+ 8	+13	+20				
33	My principal	No	−30	+13	+ 9	+10	+ 9				
47	My guest at white dance	No	−35	+ 4	+ 7	+13	+13				
49	My escort at theater	No	−30	+ 9		+13	+ 9				
50	My escort at Negro dance	No	−37	+ 4	+ 2	+15	+15				
51	My intimate chum	No	−37	+ 6	+ 6	+ 2	+22				
IIA 16	All social benefits of white man, but limited to own race	No	+37						−30	− 4	
B 4	Definite and marked differences between two races	No	+35						−39		
B 15	Not condemned forever to lower, but different, place	No	+35						−26		
B 12	The Negro, given high position in society, will prove equal to it	Yes	+33					−11			
III 2	Homes should be segregated	Disapprove	+25							−22	
IV 6	Evolution proves mating undesirable	No	+30						−32	− 6	−33

* Small shifts on responses are not always given.

TABLE IX B

CONSIDERABLE PRO-NEGRO SHIFTS MADE BY EXPERIMENTAL GROUP FROM INITIAL TEST TO RE-TEST, BY ITEMS (46 CASES)

Item No.	Item	Response on Which Shift Occurred	Percentage of Shift on Given Response	Most	Many	Some	Few	No	Yes	Uncertain	Approve	Disapprove
I 5	Same apartment house	No	−20	+ 6	+11		+ 6*					
7	Roommate	No	−26			+ 9	+15					
19	My secretary	No	−17	+ 6	+15		+ 2					
22	My business partner	No	−24	+ 6	+13							
23	My superior	No	−17	+ 6	+15	+ 6	−11					
29	My partner in dance	No	−22			+11	+ 6					
30	Member of my social set	No	−22		+ 8	+20	− 9					
37	My social group at church	No	−17	+ 6		+13	− 4					
46	My guest at theater	No	−22		+ 9	+17	− 6					
4	Same hotel	Some	−22	+11	+11							
48	My host at Negro home	Few	−20	+11	+ 9	+ 6		− 6				
IIA 15	Brothers in Christ, not in law	No	+20									
IIB 1	Many years of civilization needed to reach white social level	No	+22						−22		−15	− 4
8	Entitled to same social privileges	Yes	+22					− 9				−15

TABLE IX B—(Continued)

	Response				
III 1 Negroes would become disagreeable if not held in place	No	+20	−8	−11	
8 Treat all in the same class	Strongly disapprove	+22			−22
12 Hotel should refuse Negroes	Strongly disapprove	+26		−11	−15
IV A Address Negro as Mr. etc.	Strongly approve	+22			−17
4 Will never reach white level	No	+28	−13	−15	
7 Negro and white children educated in same school	Yes	+22	−24		
14 Complete social equality	Yes	+26	−30	+4	

* Small shifts on responses are not always given.

or anti-Negro shifts on responses given to individual items. It should be noted that these were shifts from or to a particular response on an item. If the item had been studied as a whole, the chi-square test might have been used to study the discrepancy between the responses in the first and second test. This, however, would have involved the dubious assumption that the responses on the first and second test were independent. To secure, however, a rule of thumb which would classify the items into three groups, those having a highly reliable shift on a given response, those having a fairly reliable shift, and those with negligible change, the items were treated *as though* the responses had been made by two really independent groups, and the reliability of the difference between percentages making a given response on the first and second administration was calculated. Admittedly this is only a convenient device of classification. Table IX A contains all items in which the significant ratio thus obtained is 3 or more, and Table IX B those with significant ratio less than 3 but more than 2.

No large shift of any kind as indicated by this ratio of 3 or more was found in the control group. A single case of the second category (significant ratio 2.4) was found in the control group on Item IV 10 ("Colored people are equal to whites in potential ability but have lacked opportunity"); there was an increase of 24 percent in the response "Yes" and a decrease of 15 percent in the response "Uncertain" and of 9 percent in the response "No," conceivably as a result of intervening educational experiences. No anti-Negro shifts of any amount were found in the experimental group except for half a dozen items where shifts of 2, or 4, or in one case 6 percent, took place to adjoining positions. On the other hand, thirteen very large pro-Negro shifts which in content indicated direct reduction of social distance in the most unmistakable manner were found in the experimental group.

Table IX A summarizes these results. The section "Increase or Decrease in Percentage on Certain Other Responses" is given simply to assist the reader in conjecturing what took place in the shift, by indicating where losses (or gains) were reflected in corresponding gains (or losses) in other responses which seem chargeable to this movement. In the first example (I 13), for instance, it is not to say that 20 percent who asserted on the first test that they would under *No* conditions eat at the same table with a Negro responded on the re-test that under *Many* conditions they would do so. But since *Few* and *Some* lost slightly in the same movement, there must have been a pyramiding of favorable shifts which swept the wave on to *Many*. No attempt is made to record every minor shift.

In the Acceptable Relationship Test the *No* barrier seems especially important to observe. It is certainly the most absolute position on the scale. It expresses an extreme of social distance. When, then, a highly reliable number of the members of the experimental group abandon the *No* barrier in favor of a degree of acceptance of Negroes in such personal relationships as dining, company in travel, educational leadership, recreation at theater or dance, and trusted and intimate friendship, positive changes in personal valuation of certain Negroes at least seems to have been accomplished, and a denial of various traditional ostracisms seems implicit in it. (See items in Table IX A.) This hypothesis is supported by the six significant shifts in other parts of the battery. In greater or lesser degree they all bear on the issue of segregation. In III 9 approval is explicitly withdrawn by 33 percent from segregation of Negro homes; 26 percent change their position to positive disapproval. Thirty-three percent have gained confidence that the Negro, if given a high position in society, will prove equal to it (II B 12). To 35 percent racial differences no longer seem so definite and marked (II B 4). Whether this is a case of pro-Negro prejudice, or whether it represents a new scale of human differences in which racial differences seem less important than differences of other sorts within races, it would be hard to say. Item IV 6, stating that "the doctrine of evolution proves that Negroes and Whites should not mate," is of course a test of anti-Negro prejudice, since the doctrine of evolution offers no such proof. What this statement expresses is an emotional objection to intermarriage between the races. It would of course be conceivable to conclude that 30 percent of the experimental group had awakened to the fallacy. How reasonable it is to conclude this, however, may perhaps be judged by the fact that in the large group of 354 students 29 percent held this opinion, and 29 percent were uncertain about it, while in the control group during the interim 11 percent abandoned their denial of the opinion in form of uncertainty or assent. Probably the change in response of 30 percent in the experimental group reflects feeling rather than logic, and indicates a withdrawal of another of the fear-barriers on which segregation rests. Certainly in the two remaining items (IIA 16 and IIB 15), which offer theoretically liberal compromises between social distance and the principle of equality, 35 percent and 37 percent respectively changed their vote to *No*. No shifts of attitudes perhaps are more impressive than these, representing as they do an approach to enlightened Negro opinion that equality on the social distance basis is both specious and undesirable, and that in the American scene a different, but not lower, place in which all social benefits of the white man are available within the limits of the Negro race is a logical and practical contradiction in terms.

In addition to these very large shifts of response on thirteen items the experimental group showed considerable shift of response on eighteen, or according to a more inclusive standard, twenty-one other items as indicated by the significant ratio of more than 2 and less than 3, whereas the control group showed a comparable shift of response on one item only (Table IX B). Some hesitation was felt about including III 8, III 12, and IV A in this group, since the shifts were simply from one degree of approval or disapproval to another, but since the shift was so large and apparently so clearly an indication of feeling, they were finally included. On the other hand, a strictly conservative policy was followed on such items as I 23, 30, 37, 46, and 48, where if the considerable shift from *Few* had been summed with that from *No,* a very large shift for the combination would probably have been discovered.

Little comment needs to be made upon Table IX B as it stands. The same trends are apparent as in the very large shifts. Abandonment of the *No* barrier continues in the middle ranges of current social distance where the breach with convention is less obvious, but where the importance of public opinion to the Negro's career or his mode of life is perhaps even greater; for example, in chances of employment as secretary, or of promotion as superior, in residence in the same apartment house or same hotel, or co-education in the same schools. On the issue of education, Statement IV 13 that Negro children in the public schools are able to do as good work as is done by the average white child of similar age registered an amount of shift just short of the criterion for inclusion in Table IX B; it is undoubtedly an indicator of pro-Negro prejudice as referring to present-day performance in many schools rather than to ability under equal conditions, but for this very reason it indicates a change in emotional attitude. The two highest indices belong to items calling for equal privileges and complete social equality (II B 8 and IV 18).

To sum up, out of 112 items in the battery 34 registered very large or considerable shift of response by the experimental group as against one only by the control group.

No attempt will be made to tabulate the items in which lesser shifts took place. A few pro-Negro shifts began to appear here in the control group. Eleven percent abandoned the *No* barrier in regard to resident in the same apartment house, guest in the same family, and diner at the same table. Thirteen percent shifted from *Few* to *Many* in regard to the same restaurant.

There was a 15 percent gain in approval of co-education in the same schools and an equal denial of inferiority in innate capacity. Thirteen percent more denied that there was an impassable gulf between the races, and 11 percent more asserted that if given a high position in society the Negro would show himself equal to it.

A number of shifts in the control group unfavorable to the Negro occur, however, as well, of which only a few of the more interesting will be reported. Eleven percent more on the re-test gave the response that under *No* conditions were they willing to have Negroes participate in student parties. Eleven percent formerly willing under *Many* or under *Some* conditions to have a Negro teacher in the same school now registered the conditions under which they were willing as *Few*. Thirteen percent abandoned *No* for *Uncertain* and *Yes* in regard to instinctive aversion.

The experimental group continued in this category as well to exceed the control group in number of pro-Negro shifts. Shifts between 11 and 16 percent were discovered in 36 items. Only a few of these will be mentioned. The *No* answer was totally abandoned in the items of social recognition by culture, and Negro contribution to art, the *Yes* answer was abandoned in the statement that the Negro's proper place is in manual work. In the social distance area, objection to physical proximity declined consistently in a series of items, such as same neighborhood, same street, same restaurant, same sleeping car, adjoining seat, participant in student parties, guest in the same family. Two items in the political field merit attention—lesser official and official of high rank. In the former case reductions along the entire line in every response except "under *Most* conditions" brought to *Most* an increase of 22 percent. At the same time 13 percent abandoned the *No* barrier against an official of high rank, and were supported by a decline of 15 percent from *Few* (and of 2 percent from *Some*), indicating an impressive vote of confidence in the qualifications of Negroes for public position. Eleven percent abandoned the *No* barrier against having a Negro as personal guest in their own home, and were supported by a decrease of 15 percent from *Few*. Finally, in the most socially tabooed relationships of kinship by marriage, and marriage, 15 percent and 13 percent respectively abandoned the *No* barrier in favor of the responses that under *Few* or *Some* conditions such a relationship would be acceptable.

Shifts on Individual Items Against the Background of the Large Group

Thus far the changes in attitude discovered in the experimental group have been viewed as changes within the group itself. Perspective will be gained on their general social significance by viewing them against the background of the large group of 354 students, which may tentatively be taken as a sample of somewhat liberal attitudes in wider circles. Exhaustive treatment of the attitudes will not be attempted, but the investigation will be largely confined to the social distance sphere.

Among the various relationships presented in the Acceptable Relationship Test, which ones were acceptable under few or no conditions to 35 percent or more of the large group of 354 students? Such a criterion should point out the larger gaps of social distance between white and Negro groups, and give some measure of the distance. A division of items was made according to whether the vote represented a large minority of 35–50 percent of the students, or a majority. The two groups of items are shown in Tables X and XI, with the percentage of *Few* and *No* responses combined, and of *No* responses alone. For purposes of comparison the initial and re-test percentages of the experimental group are given, as well as the percentages of gain or loss in these responses. Thus the effect of the experiment can be clearly seen against the background of the more striking current ostracisms of the Negro.

TABLE X

Less Acceptable Relationships with Negro as Defined by Adverse 35 to 50 Per Cent of Total Group, and Comparable Responses of Experimental Group Before and After Exposure

Item No.	Relationship	Total Group (N 354) Under Few or No Conditions Initial	Experimental Group (N 46) Under Few or No Conditions			Under No Conditions		
			Initial	Re-Test	Shift	Initial	Re-Test	Shift
1 2	Neighborhood	36.8	34.7	17.4	17.3	13.0	6.5	6.5
3	Street	46.4	37.0	21.7	15.3	19.5	6.5	13.1
4	Hotel	42.7	21.7	23.9	−2.2	13.0	6.5	6.5
11	Sleeping car	47.9	28.2	19.6	8.6	13.0	2.2	10.8
13	Table	49.4	41.3	17.4	23.9	21.7	2.2	19.5
19	Secretary	46.3	41.3	26.1	15.2	26.1	8.7	17.4
28	Participant student parties	34.8	30.4	21.7	8.7	15.2	4.3	10.9
37	Social group at church	45.7	41.3	19.5	21.8	23.9	6.5	17.4
42	Official of high rank	44.9	43.5	15.2	28.3	17.4	4.3	13.1
43	Protege	43.5	41.3	37.0	4.3	23.9	10.9	13.0

PERCENTAGE OF STUDENTS GIVING ADVERSE VOTE

The relationships singled out by the criterion as of moderate difficulty are in most cases those areas familiar in the news or in common experience as productive of opposition or friction. When a Negro seeks a home in a white neighborhood or on a white street, asks for a room in a hotel at which whites are guests, desires accommodation in a sleeping car, or eats at the same table in a restaurant, he has to be apprehensive of objection of a more or less positive sort from some part of the white environment. In seeking a position a qualified Negro secretary knows that a great deal of difficulty will be encountered on the grounds of race alone. Where Negroes attend churches with white people, they seldom experience genuine social equality with white people of the same interests and cultural level. That the *No* barrier is weakest in regard to participation in student parties (I28) is probably due to the influence of the special educational environment in which fewer social concomitants are involved on the one hand, and in which theories of equality are most frequently and consistently advocated and examined for their implications on the other. It is perhaps surprising that the *No* barrier against accepting a Negro as an official of high rank is so low. Negroes have frequently been selected as United States consuls to Latin American or other countries where race is not a serious obstacle, but that fact is hardly of general knowledge. The term protégé for a friendly relationship of recognized unequal status was rather ambiguous, and suffers that limitation in the discussion of it.

The two groups were not very dissimilar in their *Few* and *No* responses, and in their *No* responses, initially, particularly after the first few items. On these the experimental group is noticeably less averse on the first five items in terms of the *No* response, and on Items 3, 4, and 11 in terms of the combined responses, and in general it shows itself somewhat more accessible. While this somewhat lower degree of aversion must be taken into account in estimating the responsiveness of the experimental group to the seminar influences, it is nevertheless apparent that on the initial test the *No* barrier was high against all these relationships, while in the re-test it has practically been swept away. Only against the relationship of protégé (Item 43) is it as much as 10 percent, and this may be complicated by objection to the type of relationship as such, or to the unequal status for the Negro which is implied. The same observation is in point regarding the negligible shift on this item in the combined responses. Out of seven relationships initially, it is the only one toward which a third or more of the cases continued averse. The only other item on which the responses remained virtually unchanged was Item 4, resident in the same hotel, the relationship least objectionable at the outset and one on which the experimental group had been most liberal as against the larger group. The *No* responses, however, declined by half. Apart from protégé the only relationship out of nine at the outset which was still regarded as difficult or impossible by a fourth or more of the cases was that of secretary, and marked reduction of aversion toward this was registered both in the *No* and in the combined responses. As measured by the test, the experimental group seems to have reduced its objection to the Negro in a number of relationships in respect to which he frequently suffers discrimination.

Shifts in Respect to Least Acceptable Relationships

Eighteen relationships were under few or no conditions acceptable to an absolute majority of the larger group. Eleven of these were not acceptable to the majority under any conditions (Table XI). These are the areas in which the ostracism of the Negro can be considered greatest. Prior to the experiment the responses of the experimental group corresponded with those of the larger group with considerable fidelity. They showed rough agreement in amount; in addition, of the eighteen relationships, each exceeded the other in half (nine each on the *No*

TABLE XI

LEAST ACCEPTABLE RELATIONSHIPS WITH NEGRO AS DEFINED BY ADVERSE MAJORITY OF TOTAL GROUP, AND COMPARABLE RESPONSES OF EXPERIMENTAL GROUP BEFORE AND AFTER EXPOSURE

Item No.	Relationship	PERCENT OF 354 STUDENTS		PERCENT OF EXPERIMENTAL GROUP OF 46 STUDENTS					
		Under Few or No Conditions	Under No Conditions	Under Few or No Conditions			Under No Conditions		
				Initial	Re-Test	Shift	Initial	Re-Test	Shift
5	Apartment house	59.0	41.5	52.2	39.1	13.1	32.6	13.0	19.6
6	Family guest	58.5	36.2	50.0	43.5	6.5	21.7	8.7	13.0
7	Room-mate	85.0	72.6*	84.8	73.9	10.9	73.9	47.8	26.1
15	Stateroom on boat	76.8	64.4	82.6	63.0	19.6	69.6	30.4	39.2
22	Business partner	67.2	53.1	60.9	39.1	21.8	41.3	17.4	23.9
23	Superior	63.0	44.4	60.8	32.6	28.2	30.4	13.0	17.4
29	Partner in dance	72.1	60.2	78.3	63.0	15.2	60.9	39.1	21.8
30	Social set	71.7	52.5	76.1	45.7	30.4	47.8	26.1	21.7
33	Principal	65.3	48.9	65.2	43.5	21.7	50.0	19.6	30.4
45	Guest at my home	58.5	30.8	52.2	26.1	26.1	19.6	8.7	10.9
46	Guest at theater	64.4	42.4	63.0	34.8	28.2	32.6	10.9	21.7
47	Guest at white dance	83.9	67.5	84.8	63.1	21.7	69.6	34.8	34.8
48	Host at Negro home	58.2	30.8	50.0	23.9	26.1	15.2	8.7	6.5
49	Escort at theater	82.2	70.6	87.0	65.3	21.7	67.4	37.0	30.4
50	Escort at Negro dance	82.1	70.0	86.9	65.2	21.7	80.4	43.5	36.9
51	Intimate chum	84.1	70.0	89.1	73.9	15.2	71.7	34.8	36.9
52	Kin by marriage	95.5	88.4	97.8	84.7	13.1	95.6	80.4	15.2
53	Husband or wife	98.5	94.1	100.0	91.3	8.7	95.6	82.6	13.0

* Bold face type indicates percentages over fifty in given column.

alone, nine on *Few* plus *No*). On eight of the eleven relationships least acceptable the experimental group gave a higher percentage of *No* responses than the larger group, noticeably on Items 50 and 52, escort at Negro dance and kin by marriage. On Items 30 and 49 the correspondence was close, although on the former the percentage dropped slightly below a majority. On Item 22, that of business partner, there is a curious divergence in a pro-Negro direction by both the experimental and the control group, in neither of which did a majority find the relationship completely unacceptable. Otherwise the control group agreed almost exactly with the larger group in the amount of *No* responses on these eleven items, and remained practically constant in respect to them in the re-test. Of the seven items remaining, which less than a majority of 354 students considered completely unacceptable, the percentage of the experimental group is lower than that of the larger group on six, suggesting a somewhat greater liberality. It is interesting that in both groups the percentages are lowest in the two relationships of guest at home and host at Negro home (Items 45 and 48), in which the possibilities of privacy and freedom of choice are greatest, and that in an approximate fashion the percentages rise as one or the other factor or both diminish in the stages of guest in the same family, resident in the same apartment house, guest at theater, and superior. It suggests the notion that aversion to physical proximity or personal intimacy is not so strong as fear of being conspicuous or of attracting group censure, in holding individuals to conventional discriminations against the Negro. It is suggestive also that the smaller group conformed less on relationships lacking, and more on relationships having, complete unacceptability to the majority.

What is the situation at the end of the experiment? Nothing more dramatically suggests the effects of the experiment than the re-test percentages on these relationships indicated by the criterion as ordinarily least acceptable. Evidently the most striking changes of attitude in the experimental group were for the most part precisely in these areas of greatest difficulty, where emotional set might be expected to be strongest. Out of seven statistically significant shifts of attitude in the social distance field, as shown in Table IX A, six concern relationships at first absolutely unacceptable to half or more of the experimental group. Out of nine shifts from the *No* response whose indices of significance ranged from 2 to 3 seven took place on items in this list (Table IX B). Out of the eighteen relationships acceptable under few or no conditions to half or more of this group nine no longer attract the aversion of a majority. Of the remaining nine six registered shifts of 15 or more percent. To be sure, all continue to be areas of caution and difficulty, and on only one (Item 48, host in Negro home) has aversion as measured by the combined responses dropped below 25 percent. But for three-fourths of the group, eight instead of three relationships are now conceivable under certain conditions, and among them it is interesting to note Items 23 and 33, superior and school principal. Finally, out of nine completely unacceptable to a majority at the outset only kinship by marriage, and marriage itself, so remain. It should be pointed out that these relationships are exactly those in which qualities of personality are most involved, and in which acceptability depends most on one's valuation as a person. This evidence tends to show that a revaluation of the worth of some Negroes at least occurred.

Analysis of Responses to Attitude Statements

Of the 61 attitude statements in the rest of the test battery, 13 could be classified as occupying a middle ground. On 35 of the 48 remaining, a majority of 354 students gave responses favorable to the Negro with various percentages of agreement, answering *No* to hostile statements and *Yes* to favorable statements. This may indicate the relative liberality of the group in another fashion. On three favorable and four hostile statements there were roughly equal percentages answering *Yes, Uncertain,* and *No.* The favorable statements were II 3, IV 7, and IV 13, which assert that if given a high status in society the Negro will prove equal to it, that Negro and white children should be educated in the same schools, and that Negro children are capable of as good work in school as white children. The hostile statements were IV 4, IV 9, IV 6, and IV 5, which assert that the Negro will never reach the white level, that he is inferior in innate capacity, that the doctrine of evolution proves there should be no intermarriage, and that Negro leaders are almost invariably of mixed blood and owe their qualities to their white ancestry. In general, the experimental and control groups showed remarkably close initial resemblance to the parent group of 354 on the distribution of responses, but in all but one of these statements the experimental group shifted sufficiently to give a majority to the pro-Negro response in the re-test. The striking example is IV 5, the last statement mentioned, in which one person only changed from *No* to *Uncertain,* and another from *No* to *Yes.* Evidently the Harlem experiences had little or no effect on the generalization that Negro leaders are almost invariably of mixed blood, and owe their qualities to their white ancestry. This agrees with testimony from the interviews which tended to show that the group was more surprised at the realization that American Negroes are a mixed group than at the abilities of those speakers and acquaintances of the seminar who were markedly Negroid.

On five statements the majority of the total group gave responses unfavorable to the Negro, approving three hostile statements, and denying two favorable statements. Fifty-six percent asserted a difference not merely in degree but in kind between the two races, 52 percent maintained that there would always be an impassable gulf, 62 percent approved of segregation of homes, 54 percent disapproved of complete social equality. The other statement (II A2), that the educated Negro is less of a burden on the courts than the educated white man, no doubt an expression of pro-Negro prejudice, was denied by 68 percent.

General comparison of the experimental and control group on this body of 61 attitude statements was not attempted, but striking differences in shifts on the re-test were found on certain interesting questions, which are not always the same as the outstanding gains within the experimental group, because of simultaneous movements in a positive or negative direction in the control group.

Nine of such differences in shift were found. Since they add nothing new to the discussion, they will not be tabulated, but simply summarized. Three concerned segregation (III 9; II A16; IIB 15). One concerned equality of privileges (IV 14). Three concerned equality of capacity (IV 4; II B1; II B5). Two concerned intermarriage (IV 6; II 15).

In this section of this volume a general picture of the prevailing situation has now been given from the test results against which the pertinence of the present experiment may be estimated. The analysis of test results as a whole, which will be summarized in a later chapter, tends to support the conclusion that measurable changes in attitude were effected in the experimental group by the Harlem experiment.

V: Supplementary Evidence Bearing
on the Experiment

THREE sources furnish a certain amount of supplementary evidence as to the effects of the experiment. Listing them in the reverse of chronological order, they are (1) the second re-tests, administered to the experimental and control groups by mail ten months or more after the first re-test, to measure the degree of permanence of the gains, (2) individual interviews two months after the first re-test to secure data on the individual's earlier experience, attitudes during the tests and seminar, and belief as to score on the first re-test, and (3) attendance at a voluntary tea at Columbia University, about one month after the first re-test, for Harlem acquaintances and hosts who had contributed to the seminar.

The Tea

Apart from the fact that the tea may have had a certain influence on the interviews and the final re-tests, it perhaps need not have been mentioned. Thanks to the hospitality of a chaplain of the University, who contributed the meeting-place, refreshments, and musical program, it was possible to invite together the members of the seminar, and any friends they might choose to bring, for informal social conversation at tea with many of the personalities with whom the seminar had supplied contact, and with members of their families. Approximately seventy people were present, including personal guests of members, in roughly equal numbers from the racial point of view. Twenty-six members of the seminar were present, and at least eight others, four of whom had accepted the invitation, were absent from causes beyond their control. This is a very satisfactory response under metropolitan conditions to a bare post-card announcement at short notice. The twelve members of the seminar remaining to be accounted for include the individual with the lowest score both for the total and for the Acceptable Relationship Test on all three administrations, the individual who withdrew from the seminar because of public opinion hostile to it, three individuals whose exposure to the seminar was amputated, and the individual with the second lowest total score on the three administrations, and the second lowest score for the Acceptable Relationship Test on the two re-tests. Three others were of Southern origin and upbringing, one had been cut by acquaintances for membership in the seminar, and one was a person of heavy professional responsibility, who is unaccounted for. One other member was absent for reasons unknown. These may of course only be plausible coincidences, and should not be pressed. The tea was not planned in any sense as a measuring device of readinesses, old or new, for experiences of social equality with Negroes but as a bona fide expression of appreciation for hospitality in Harlem. Nevertheless, in retrospect it seems capable of gauging roughly the extent to which certain types of social equality with Negroes were now acceptable after an interval of six weeks, and to be suggestive of various similar means using more careful and scientific procedure, for measuring the acquisition of new adjustments and drives in the social field, and if properly refined even measuring their force. This whole field of possibility, however, had to remain totally unexplored.

The Interviews

Forty-five individual interviews were secured two months or more after the first re-test, and consisted of informal conversations lasting generally half an hour and incorporating the following questions:

1. Please rank the three sections of the Harlem program you appreciated most, and the three you appreciated least. Why did you choose these?

2. What previous experiences of yours resembled any experiences of the seminar? What new experiences, if any, did the seminar present to you?

3. What surprises, annoyances, conflicts, or thrills, if any, do you recall?

4. What has been your acquaintance with Negroes in the past? Please give details.

5. Do you recall ever changing your attitude toward Negroes at any time? What were the particular incidents apparently involved? What groups to which you have belonged differed most in their attitude toward the Negro?

6. In what ways, if any, has the Harlem experience been of value to you?

7. What activities, if any, involving Negroes or your racial attitudes have you engaged in since the seminar? Reading? Meetings? New acquaintances? New relationships? Defense of your opinions? Please give details.

8. What feelings did you have toward taking the first test? The second test? Do you think you changed your score on the second test?

Answers were taken down in longhand verbatim at the time with as great fullness as possible, and were not revised. Some relatively minor omissions may have occurred, but substantial accuracy of quotation was obtained.

In discussing the evidence of these necessarily subjective interviews, it is difficult to avoid reporting either too much or too little. The striking variety of local tradition and custom in various localities of the United States, which conventional generalizations of sectional opinion miss entirely, idiosyncrasies of individual experience in home, childhood history, school, college, travel, and accidental contacts, the personal preferences and aversions toward specific Harlem experiences, and the particular symbolic forms in which advance toward (or retreat from) the Negro group were expressed, form a varied and kaleidoscopic picture. Since, however, the present study is focused on the experimental production of changes in attitude, the interviews will be utilized here chiefly to obtain from the experimental subjects' introspective analysis an idea of the effect of the experimental factor on their attitudes, and to secure evidence bearing on the validity of the test findings.

Degree of Sophistication

In estimating the meaning of the experimental gains, assuming for the moment that the test results are valid, it is valuable to know to what degree unusual impressionability and lack of experience account for the changes and to what degree prior experiences of Negroes served to balance the exposure to superior Negro individuals and cultural groups. Of course most determinative contacts with members of one's own group are with those of one's own cultural level, and it is generally tacitly assumed that judgment of other dominant peoples should be determined in the same way. Bias is evident when Oriental and other colored peoples are estimated on other principles. In any case: what levels of experience existed in the group, speaking generally?

It may be recalled that the group consisted of mature students with a mean age of approximately thirty-three. The interviews showed that they were brought up in the following types of communities: 9 in big cities, 6 in suburban communities, 5 in large towns of 10,000 or more, 9 in small towns, and 16 in villages of 2,000 or less or in rural districts. Only one was brought up in New York City, but it is noteworthy that this student not only made striking and progressive gains in score throughout the first and second re-test, but led in actual establishment of new social adjustments during the succeeding year. On the other hand, another individual from a small Southern town who had suffered from fear of Negroes until maturity, made as striking gains from a lower initial score, and successfully initiated the next year high school study of local Negro problems there.

One reason for the small number of local representatives was undoubtedly the fact that invitations to the seminar were not sent to suburban commuters, as was explained. Most of the students in the experiment were residents of university dormitories or near-by apartments.

In terms of prior acquaintance with Negroes the group might be distributed as follows: 14 had had Negro servants regularly, 6 occasionally, 5 had had Negro neighbors, 5 not thus far mentioned had had Negro friends as equals, 15 had had scant contacts with Negroes during youth, 4 of whom had known a good many later in the capacity of pupils or fellow students, 1 had had extended unpleasant contacts with stevedores in a navy yard, and several of the others had attended school or college where a few Negroes were students without making them personal acquaintances. Four of those listed as having had Negroes as servants knew Negroes also as friends and equals. Four members had traveled abroad, one of whom had been an official in Haiti.

Some Cases of Negative Conditioning

An approximate classification on the basis of mind-set toward the Negro prior to the experiment would probably show the following: 8 favorable, 9 indifferent, 8 naive, 5 unfavorable, and 15 mixed. Among the mixed cases were a few extremely interesting examples of negative conditioning. At the age of seven one individual felt great fear at the unusual sight of a tall Negro approaching on the street, although the fear was not shared by an accompanying cousin. Though Negroes were few, aversion continued so intense that some years later the individual could not endure taking hold of hands in a gymnasium class in which two or three Negro girls were members. This person's sister did not share this feeling. Prior to the seminar this person had never shaken hands with a Negro, and felt an aversion to entering the residence club where the first speech of the seminar took place. Only the presence of the group enabled the entry to be made. The feeling was gone, however, by supper time, when the Y. W. C. A. was entered.

Another individual from a border state had represented a college society at an international conference. While eating with some Japanese girls she saw a Negro girl sit down at the same table. She immediately rose and finished her meal standing, to the surprise of the Japanese. In the realm of symbolic action, eating with Negroes was for her the chief adjustment of the seminar, and at the social party this person even lent assistance in serving the refreshments. For certain other members dread of shaking hands which was postponed until the occasion made avoidance awkward, dread of eating at the same table, of entering a private home, or of accepting the relationship of guest of the owner of an automobile were present beforehand, and successfully dissipated as the seminar developed.

If the group had at least a normal amount of resistance to over-exaggerated response because of negative experiences, the same may be held true of favorable experiences. Various members had heard Negro speakers, attended Negro concerts, read Negro poetry, seen Negro plays, attended Negro churches, entertained Negro guests, had friendly dealings with Negroes in the business world. One individual on a certain voyage had adjusted cabins to secure as roommate a well-liked Negro friend rather than a white stranger.

The Seminar Experienced as "New"

A surprise of the interviews was that by a large majority the seminar was experienced as "all new," or "practically all new," even by individuals who in analyzing their past gave unmistakable evidence of extensive contacts with Negroes in ways comparable in many details with Harlem events. The reason seems to have been twofold, first, the quality of the persons and groups experienced, and second, the integration of the elements into a cumulative unity within a great Negro community, what might be called the Gestalt of the experience (27:128). Discussing the second point first, the progressive rise to new social adjustments and the release from narrow inhibitions were sufficiently gradual and well motivated and supported by the environing group of students to seem natural and possible. Illustrations of this have already been given. The value of this cumulative arrangement may perhaps be seen also by its absence in the case of certain individuals who missed the integration. Two people were prevented by professional duties at the last moment from starting with the group the first day, thus missing the adjustments involved, and the influence of personalities and subject matter chosen for their universal appeal. One of the two henceforth avoided all meals and most social events at which Negroes might be expected, remained merely a spectator, and in particular suffered marked irritation at the more outspoken character of later speakers. "I felt I had had too much of it, couldn't have gone further with it." The other, less inhibited, attended the social service luncheon, but omitted the other experiences alluded to, and was obviously not drawn forward by the developing process. Another bit of testimony to the value of integration may be found in the following quotations from students who noted it in contrast to other experiences, even including hearing some of the speakers of the seminar elsewhere. Elsewhere "the lectures were just like any lectures. Off in the distance. Remote. Nothing to do with you. When they are not on their own ground, you feel they are defending them." "This speech [elsewhere] was entirely intellectual. Mr. —— was equally good in both of them, but in one you sit as the audience, while in the other you are part of the cast." "I went into it from curiosity, as an adventure. By Sunday night everything was different. The first week-end caused a revolution in my mind. Mr. ——'s talk made you feel here was someone worth listening to. . . . There wouldn't have been the same feeling and atmosphere in a lecture hall." "It's one thing to hear about a thing, and it's another to see it, experience it." "I liked the idea of the continuity running through." Another, referring to a shorter previous trip to Harlem, said, "But that was more on the outside."

Turning from form to content in this experience of "newness," students concurred in their analyses with an approach to unanimity which was noteworthy. A few quotations from students with initial low, average, and high scores will sufficiently illustrate these characterizations. The first are from those with low scores. "I never before had contacts with intellectual and cultured Negroes, only servants." "I had never seen people of that sort before." "I didn't realize that in a Negro church you could have such an atmosphere of culture and refinement. . . . I never enjoyed any day more than that Sunday. Not one syllable was uttered that reminded me of the typical Negro people of the South. . . . I can hold that Sunday as a picture to visualize before me any time in the future. I don't think —— or —— (two nationally known New York preachers) have much on him" (referring to the minister heard). "I had felt I was as good as any nigger. Now I'm taken down a peg, feel to a good many I am inferior. . . . I was thrilled at ——'s home. They had the most charming manners of any people I ever met in my life. . . . I feel a good many are much broader minded than most people, even the bitter ones." "I was impressed all through with the type of intellect we met with. . . . I had never met any Negroes like that. . . . I had heard about them, but never realized they existed until I'd come in contact with a Negro who could really show me up, like ——."

From students of average scores came remarks like the following. "I had never met so high a type of Negro. For the first time I was conscious of Negro superiority, all-round superiority of certain individuals, in which it was impossible to find any ways in which they weren't superior." "I had a feeling at —— that they had finer natures than we had, that we didn't stand out so tall. —— [the speaker on another occasion] was a marvellous combination of intellect, culture, and fineness." "I think this has given me an entirely different idea of Negro life and of the possibilities of the Negro. They are rapidly coming into their own." (Student with score somewhat above average.)

It would be tedious to extend these illustrations. A last quotation may be included from an individual of high academic standing, wide acquaintance of the world, and critical judgment. For him the personally new experiences were "(1) the Negro church service, (2) the entertainment in a private automobile owned by a Negro, (3) meeting a Negro scholar of the type of ——, (4) eating in a Negro cafeteria with a largely Negro constituency, (5) the social party in a sophisticated Negro home, and (6) accepting hospitality of a group like the college women's sorority." The values gained were "new experiences, sounder information, increased perspective, certain modifications on the ideological level, e.g., with respect to intermarriage, though with a question just how much shift on level of personal actions and reactions. New awareness of the outstanding capacity of certain Negroes and of their apparently complete freedom from any attitude of subservience or inferiority. New friends." "I was challenged to easy acceptance of what other people think is good for the Negro rather than letting him speak for himself. I met unusually competent individuals more than a match for myself and many of my white friends—also individuals representing in themselves the kind of intelligent self-respect that a wise handling of the Negro problem should result in."

From this cursory survey it seems legitimate to conclude that the interviews tend to corroborate the test analyses in discovering a group trend toward a higher valuation of certain Negroes, associated evidently with considerable emotional satisfaction and a higher expectation of Negro acceptability in personal relations.

Negative Influences

Testimony as to *individual* changes in attitude, in distinction from the trend of the group, could conceivably be presented in various ways. Perhaps the most fruitful will be to attempt to compare this testimony with individual score phenomena. First, however, negative or arresting influences of the seminar on the attitudes of a few individuals should be mentioned. In some cases the effects were due to a personal realization for the first time of the existence and extent of a Negro problem, in others to the discovery of the peril of intermarriage, less decisively the strength of Negro protest at the status quo, or the reserve and social self-sufficiency of certain advanced Negro groups. Some individuals became aware, too, of distinct preferences in the matter of shades of color and personal appearance. The influence of hitherto latent hostile opinion among white associates cannot be overlooked.

Examples of the operation of these factors can in general be reserved until the comparison with individual scores, but one or two illustrations will be useful here. One person from an unusually liberal home and college, who had had many social contacts with Negroes in the past, said, "I would deny privileges to Negroes more consistently than previously for fear of intermarriage." Another, reporting a great deal more respect for Negroes from the seminar, said, "Yet I almost wish I hadn't gone. I began to realize it as a real problem. Formerly it was not such an impossible problem. . . . I felt it my duty to be kind and considerate, and treat them professionally. . . . Now I see the issue of social equality beyond. I can't take things like that lightly. I feel a certain resentment that it's a problem there, and I've got to do something about it." Sensing in a certain social event a feeling of intrusion and failure to achieve "genuine social interaction," another commented, "This is not to imply that I would have left it out of the experience series. The very fact of these reactions suggests it as a 'critical area,' and consequently needing subsequent exposures before completely reciprocal rapport and respect is obtained. As it was, I felt it a bit stiff, and more apt to bring the shift to a standstill than to stimulate further shift. Such periods of reconsideration may be valuable in avoiding a sentimental swing of the prejudice pendulum to the positive pole on ideal rather than real grounds." While a number felt this reserve also, others found the experience quite the opposite, promoting social ease and naturalness.

Since intermarriage is mentioned as an issue occasionally in the interview citations that follow, it may be useful to point out that it is a theoretical question rather than a "live hypothesis" with the individuals personally. Nevertheless its importance should not be underestimated, because a positive or negative feeling reaction toward it as a conception not only seems to control the presence or absence of a civilized attitude toward partners of an occasional mixed marriage, an attitude which it would probably be agreed a humane and sophisticated education would regard as a desirable achievement, but also organizes and rationalizes attitudes toward granting or denying a whole range of important but less intimate rights and privileges inherently bound up with the effective practice of theories of democracy and equality under modern conditions. In other words, the importance of the attitude toward intermarriage, so far as it concerns actual social conditions and consequently education, is not at the focus, where it seems at first sight, but somewhere out on the periphery.

It is perhaps hardly necessary to remind the reader that the quotations reflect the subject's mind more accurately than they always do the actual emphases and events of the seminar; also that in certain cases the individual's testimony as to his own attitude is conflicting. It would seem that when stereotypes are broken up, sometimes the change of feeling is recognized, while the former verbal formulations are maintained; sometimes on the contrary a change of intellectual position is expressed, while the corresponding feeling lags; and sometimes a certain bewilderment is produced both in feeling and in verbal generalization prior to reorganization on the old or new basis.

One further insertion can best be added here in order to make intelligible the classification of test cases which will be used for comparison with interview evidence. That is the data on permanence of gain. How far did the gains discovered in the first re-test persist in the second re-test ten months later?

Permanence of Gain

Re-tests were secured by mail from the experimental and control groups in response to a letter sent out ten months after the first re-test requesting cooperation in the final stages of a study of students' attitudes, and asking for the filling out of the test battery *in accordance with one's present standpoint.* Requests were made as well for (1) check marks against relationships on the Acceptable Relationship Test which had been experienced in the interim, which should be encircled if the relationship was considered new in the individual's experience; (2) specific indications of any influences tending to confirm or change one's feelings toward Negroes since the previous test; and (3) one's present reactions in retrospect to the types of contacts with Negroes experienced the previous year in New York City. These three requests brought relatively scanty returns, but a very satisfactory response was secured to the request for the re-tests. Forty-two members of the control group, and 45 members of the experimental group out of 46, returned tests. The only member of the experimental group failing to reply was absent in a country at war in the Far East. One other member failed to return the test in time for use in calculation, but 40 of the original pairs were secured.

Table XII exhibits the differences found between the initial test and the second re-test means, and their statistical significance. It will be observed that statistically significant gains persisted in four of the six measures, notably in the total battery

TABLE XII

Significance of Differences Between Second Re-Test Means of Paired Experimental and Control Group Cases (40 Pairs)

Second Re-Test After Year Interval

Part	Title	$Mean_{Exp.} - Mean_{Con.}$	$S.E._{Diff.}$	$\dfrac{Diff.}{S.E._{Diff.}}$
I	Smith	19.30	5.73	3.37
II A	Thurstone A	4.42	1.84	2.40
II B	Thurstone B	6.70	1.88	3.56
III	Murphy	2.28	.57	4.00
IV	Miscellany	1.98	.81	2.44
	Total Battery	36.15	7.63	4.74

with its index of 4.74, and that in Thurstone Form A and in the Miscellany the approach to statistical significance was close. In comparison with Table V, which presented the differences between the initial and the first re-test, there is a decrease in means and in indices of significance in every case except the Murphy-Likert test, which attained a statistically significant figure of 4.00 in this re-test.* Thus the effect of the experiment on the group as a whole diminished perceptibly, in ten months' time, but was still very strong. The experimental gain of this group as a whole has been largely permanent. It will be interesting now to examine the record of individual cases.

Classification of Individual Cases by Changes in Score

In the first re-test forty individuals increased their score in varying amounts up to 114 points. (Minor fluctuations of 10

* It should be noted that some reduction of the indices is of course due to the reduction in the number of the pairs from 46 to 40.

points or less are disregarded in this analysis.) Three fell 30 to 40 points each. Three remained approximately stationary; one of these went abroad later and failed to return a second re-test. Of the forty whose scores gained on the first re-test, 8 showed on the second re-test a further gain, 17 held their gain, 8 fell less than halfway, 2 fell more than halfway, 4 fell back to the initial score, and one fell 52 points below the initial score. One of the stationary cases remained stationary; the other showed a small gain of 20 points. Of the three who fell, one returned halfway to the initial score, one remained stationary, one showed a considerable second fall. Four cases then stood below their initial score on the second re-test by 18, 40, 52, and 88 points respectively. These cases will receive special attention later. Twenty-five held their gain or advanced.

If classified on the basis of the Acceptable Relationship Test alone, some slight changes in personnel would occur, and four additional categories would be needed. This test was somewhat more searching in its discrimination of cases than the total battery, and shifts in terms of its measurements will be pointed out at special points. Even on this test 15 cases held their gains, and 5 others increased them.

EVIDENCE OF ATTITUDES GAINED FROM INTERVIEWS COMPARED WITH BEHAVIOR IN TEST TOTAL SCORES

Some Cases Showing Successive Gains

A case rising from a low score to the mean; then well above the mean.

We* have discussed *pro* and *con* [whether to talk about this Harlem experience back home or not]. Shall I talk about it, and what viewpoint shall I take? The Negro in the upper groups has made a distinct contribution and we ought not to let this waste go on [through neglect of Negro education]. We ought to let our

* In this one case wife and husband were both in the experiment.

Negroes through education contribute economically, culturally, etc. . . . I'm a lot more sensitive now as a result of this experiment. . . .

When the test was first announced to me, I had the attitude that this test was given to check up on my attitude to the Negroes in the class with us. (I thought to myself) I must realize I'm in New York, so I answered some of these questions what I considered liberal. . . . The second time I answered on the basis of what had actually happened to me. . . . I know I changed in that hand shaking because I changed in those associations. I think I changed in my attitude toward having them as guests. . . . My two days' experience down there has been more valuable to me than several courses because I was dealing with people. . . . That lady's saying, "Would you accept us emotionally (as well as intellectually) struck me like a bomb, with people whom I hadn't regarded as capable of challenging me."

[Ten months later.] I have just completed a unit of work with a group of High School students in which I attempted to build up some racial attitudes. . . . We visited the schools and talked and played with the Negroes. As a result one High School girl said, "Why they talk just like we do, and I am in favor of inviting the Negro High School students to visit us at our school." The students are making great plans to receive the Negro students, because of the kind reception that we received. . . . I have done some work toward starting a Boy Scout troop among the Negroes.

A case near the mean, rising to a high score, and then to one of the highest.

I always thought that mulattoes were the most intelligent, but seeing ———— and his sharp and stimulating discussion my attitude toward the darker strain changed. . . . Formerly due to home influences, I was slightly prejudiced. Now it has faded down. I was more liberal, and gave more careful answering on the second test, especially when it came to close relations. I probably changed score on living in the same house, making friends, etc.

[Ten months later.] My attitude toward Negroes' intelligence, creativeness, and equality with the white race has been confirmed. [Reports considerable systematic reading, attendance of plays, attendance at Negro club meetings, social activities, etc.] . . . I feel that many people attain their attitudes concerning Negroes from hearsay, and that what is sorely needed to correct such an impression is to have these people meet the true exponents of Negro intelligence, inherent abilities, and creativeness.

A case with low score, rising well above the mean, and increasing.

It was the personalities who interested me. . . . Difference in Negro society as in white society hit me hardest. . . . The first week-end caused a revolution in my mind. . . . I am more courteous toward, and have a more vital interest in, Negro students at Teachers College. . . . I changed answers on the test *No* to *Few*. I'm not a radical even now.

[Ten months later.] It was the first time I met superior Negroes equal to leaders of the whites.

A case with low score, approaching the mean, and then high above it.

I can best summarize: I never saw in my whole experience of it that they were any different from white people. The same proportion of élite with just as fine aesthetic and artistic appreciation.

The whole New York experience showed the possibilities and limits toward which you could bring the Negro race, that Negroes can profit by an education, an idea I'll find hard to advance in the South.

I probably did change, whether due to average or chance, but I suspect due to Harlem. . . . In developing one's philosophy such experiences are basic.

[Ten months later.] I have had a strengthening of opinions shaky at the time.

A case with low score, slightly rising, and then high above the mean.

I knew I was prejudiced. . . . I can tell I have become more liberal-minded. Well, my opinions had changed by the time of the second test. On the question "Would you dance," I felt there were some Negroes in certain places with whom I would dance. . . . I believe I am more sympathetic to the Negro. . . . Well, I had never seen people of that sort before.

[Ten months later.] Since I last took this test, I made some individual and group contacts in Harlem. Now that I know more about the educated Negro, I am more sympathetic and appreciative of him than I formerly was. My prejudices are slowly dropping away. I am now able to think of the Negro in terms other than "the good old faithful servant," and the "good-for-nothing nigger." Reading, concerts, discussions with both Northerners and Southerners have widened my horizon, thereby increasing my tolerance.

A case near the mean, rising twice by moderate amounts.

It afforded my first opportunity of seeing the best the Negro had produced . . .
I don't know that the Harlem trip affected my score.

[Ten months later.] Since living in New York I have become aware of the fact that Negroes feel quite keenly that they are discriminated against. I was somewhat surprised to find that many of them have faced the problem with a great deal of intelligence.

A case with low score, rising to the mean, and then somewhat above it.

The biggest thing I got out of it was realization that the Negroes were human. I formerly looked at them from outside, with no particular hostility, but with [complete indifference].

[Ten months later.] Acquaintance with two fellow students had increased respect.

A case with high score, rising twice to one of the highest.

Intermarriage is still a question in mind, although I am specializing in biology. Jennings says it would be race suicide for the whites, but that is based purely on opinion. . . . I have more respect since this trip. . . . Probably some little prejudice [formerly] due to public opinion. Now I go out of my way not to hurt colored people's feelings. I have greater tolerance . . . and realize that they are human beings like other people. I was conscious of this particularly at ———. On the second test I knew at the time I had changed some answers.

[Ten months later. No statement.]

Cases Registering Gain, Then Stationary

A case with low initial score rising to a high score.

I can feel that my whole attitude was different, is different, since. . . . *Few* in the first test became *Many* in the second. . . . What

I liked [were the opportunities to] sit down and talk with them just as white people. Going to ———'s home, all the telephone calls just like any minister's home. ——— telling about the struggle for good schools, just as interested as other folks in good education. . . . These contacts made me conscious of many of their problems to which I had never given a thought before. . . . I had been very indifferent to them. . . . I knew very little about the facts as presented from the Negroes' side.

A case with high score rising by small increments to the highest.

New awareness of the oustanding capacity of certain Negroes.
[Ten months later.] No particular experiences except occasional personal contact with certain superior Negro students whose achievement and ability I like to see because they give the lie to many of the common prejudices against Negroes . . . often Negro friends enriched my experience fully as much or even more than many of my white friends.

A case with score just below the mean, rising to a moderate height.

This trip put away all barriers. . . . Now when I see a Negro, they are more of a personal interest to me as a person. I don't put them all in the same class any more. The other night a white fellow resented dreadfully [the presence of a Negro student at a student dance] . . . I realized while talking how differently I felt since going to Harlem. . . . I had no idea what their problems were until put by ——— and ———. . . . This experience I count as one of the big things I have had in New York.

[Ten months later.] I am still most grateful for the Harlem experience, and count it as one of my most enlightening ones. . . . I find it a strong factor in the synthesis of philosophy from day to day. . . . I was pleased recently to note my [approval of a recent speaker] for reminding us that the color line could not and would not be automatically erased; it requires special attention.

A case slightly above the mean, rising to moderate height.

No particular change in attitude. . . . If I had recalled my answers, I would have tried to be consistent.

[Ten months later.] Undoubtedly I have become more tolerant toward Negroes, as I think I have toward people in general. . . . I find that where I do meet Negroes I feel personally no . . . social superiority on account of color or race. I am sure I should resent having a white snub a black, socially.

A case about the mean, rising to a high score.

Generally we think of them all as a class. Now I think of them as individuals who can be on the level of any of us. . . . [Negroes should have all the privileges of others], but I'm confused about intermarriage. . . . I had always felt that Negroes were repulsive to me, but I don't feel like that now. . . . When I see Negroes in the library, I look at them with a new point of view. . . . I was surprised here to find there was so much opposition to getting one's point of view accepted. . . . I no longer feel any condescension.

[Ten months later.] I feel that it was a rare privilege for me to experience the contact with Negroes which I did last year. It helped me to see and think of Negroes as individuals, and not collectively which I had previously done. I feel that we came in contact with Negroes who possessed a high degree of intelligence and all that goes with it, and that they should be given equal opportunity with the same class of whites. Many of the personalities we met stand out vividly in my memory for their cleverness, charm, intellect, wit, and humor, their ability along different lines.

A case with moderately high score, rising to very high score.

I had never really and truly appreciated the sort of thing that ———— presented. The thing that was so upsetting was if that could happen to a person like ————, what could happen to someone less able. . . .

I had never experienced this sort of Negro people, . . . previously. You hear things: you don't disbelieve them, you don't believe them. Now I read articles on the intelligence of the Negro from a lot different point of view.

[Ten months later.] I don't think I am so impersonal toward the whole thing as I was. . . . I see no reason why a Negro should receive any different treatment or consideration than a white person under the same conditions.

A case with moderately high score, rising moderately.

Harlem itself was the great surprise. I had never thought of it as a community. . . . It gave me a knowledge of what they have contributed, a cleaning up of the idea that there is really no difference, only the results of oppression. . . . I didn't realize race relations were quite such a problem until I came. . . . I don't know whether my answers changed or not. There is no place where I changed my answers consciously. . . . Perhaps there was a strengthening. . . . This sort of thing is a thing we want in education.

[Ten months later.] It all depends on the personality, not the color.

All the cases in this division thus far have shown the same score movements in the Acceptable Relationship Test as well.

A case with moderately high score and small rise.

I wondered why a second test. How on earth could you change your mind as quickly as all this?

[Ten months later.] I believe I am more aware now than previous to the survey of intolerance in the attitude of white people toward colored people. [Some recent examples] seem to me to be both unintelligent and snobbish. And it annoys me.

A case with moderately high score and small rise.

The first week-end I drew the line at intermarriage and so wanted to draw the line at other things. The second week-end I was ready to conceive it, not necessarily only with the light-colored. . . . Wherever it has been a personal social thing, I've changed. . . . I wouldn't have believed when starting out on the first week-end that I could have changed so fast on so important a point. Now apart from social ostracism I would have no objection if my daughter married a Negro.

[Ten months later.] I think of Negroes entirely regardless of color—they are simply people.

A case with moderately high score and small rise.

No sudden surprises. Surprises afterwards. Direct opposition here. I had never met people before who were so fixed and hostile. . . . Harlem has brought the problem very keenly of intermarriage. I don't believe in intermarriage. I would deny privileges to Negroes more consistently for fear of intermarriage.

The last re-test and its accompanying statement indicate, not as is suggested above, withdrawal to a more restricted contact, but the establishment of a very clear line of equal social comradeship, excluding carefully the social relationships tending toward marriage. In terms of the Acceptable Relationship Test there was first a rise from, then a drop below, the initial position.

A case with moderately low score rising slightly to a point below the mean.

I felt surprise that the race had done more than we think it had. . . . I suppose it's just that color. You just throw up your hands. . . . I do feel sorry for them. . . . Harlem is wonderful over there. I feel that's the best solution, that gives them an opportunity.

In terms of the Acceptable Relationship Test the score was first stationary, followed by a considerable drop.

A case with high score, rising slightly.

I had never met this type of colored people in the United States. I was once told: "When you cross a nigger with a Frenchman, you've got quite a different breed than when you cross a nigger with an Englishman." . . . This trip proved to my satisfaction that there isn't anything to that, that it's a matter of opportunity and education.

A case with low score, rising slightly.

[No interview.]

[Ten months later.] I was very favorably impressed by the Negroes whom we met last year, but felt that most of their outstanding individuals showed evidence of having white blood in their veins. I realize that I have contradicted myself many times over in the test, but my "mind" and my "feelings" refuse to agree on the subject.

A case with moderately low score, rising close to the mean.

Until meeting with this group, we felt that the Northern Negro was officious, rather gloried in putting himself forward. . . . It [the seminar] was a thing apart from anything I ever imagined. It was a complete revelation to me. . . . The first Negro I was introduced to I was self-conscious in shaking hands with her. I was definitely aware of doing something unusual. After that you sort of got into the spirit of the thing, and forgot it. Throughout the whole thing I had this feeling of amazement, what a difference education and culture could make, that it seemed to break whatever prejudice I must have. . . . I don't think the Harlem seminar made the slightest difference in my attitude except that every opportunity should be given for education and culture. At home I just couldn't tell it. It wouldn't be convincing that it's not a matter of color, but of culture, and refinement.

[Ten months later.] Since making the trip to Harlem last spring my interest has been awakened in the activities of the Negro race. I am on the alert to read of their achievements. I have questioned a few Negroes in my home town since our return concerning their reactions to opportunities afforded them for growth mentally, socially, etc. I was amazed at the replies of our gardener, an uneducated man. I enjoyed the experience of discovering an individual. Had it not been for the Harlem trip it would never have occurred to me to see in ——— an individuality. . . . This group [of intellectuals] disproved any preconceived ideas that might have existed in our minds that the Negro as a race is not capable of mental development.

A case below the mean, rising to a moderately high score.

I don't know any one thing that I profited by so much since I have been here as this. . . . On the second test I wondered what I had said on the first one. I felt more inconsistent. I wasn't settled enough. . . . I never connected the test and the trip.

A case moderately above the mean, rising to a high score.

I did not appreciate the great similarity of interests that exists between the Negro and the white person. I had felt that because the physical barriers limited them in these United States, cultural barriers also would lessen his chances of being a person one would respect, but I found that cultural barriers have not existed as I had thought. . . . I think my score changed, although I do not believe it showed the lessening of prejudice so much as actually happened. I had intellectually rid myself of many prejudices, but the seminar rid them emotionally for me far beyond my expectations.

A case with low score, rising to the mean.

I remember the usual scares. We are warned against Negroes very often. . . . There are occasionally assaults by Negroes and then they'd be lynched. . . . It didn't at all seem new . . . except the visits to the home, and the contacts with a cultured class. . . . I think I lost myself at the home of ———. At other times I felt like a spectator. . . . I conversed with ——— forgetting that we were different. . . . It made me stop to analyze my attitude. Formerly I was just unconscious of them as hewers of wood and drawers of water. I'd never called a Negro girl Miss, or a Negro man Mr. It was always considered ordinary and common. . . . The first time the answers were emotional and highly prejudiced. The second was still full of inconsistencies and great conflict.

[Ten months later.] During the Harlem seminar last year, I came into contact for the first time with Negroes of a superior caliber. I visited a Negro home for the first time,—that is, a Negro home that approximated a white home in every way,—decoration, evidences of culture, good breeding, etc. . . . Intellectually, I realize that Negroes can be ranged along a scale just as white persons can —from very inferior to very superior. [Formerly I confess I "lumped" Negroes—regardless of quality into one group.] But emotionally I'm afraid that I have not grown up to the point of overcoming the prejudice, which having been reared in the south, would preclude my enjoying close personal relations.

This case did not start out with the group, and missed many parts of the program.

Cases Showing Gain, Later Reduced Less than Half

A case with moderately high score, rising to one of the highest, and dropping to end high.

It was a new experience feeling that they are intellectual equals, people who write books, write music. I went into the seminar expecting to find things different, and didn't. This was a surprise. I was surprised there is so much thought about the racial problem as there is. Instead of avoiding it, they were speaking about it openly and expecting you to do the same. The height of pleasure was at ——— [his conversation was so stimulating] and at ——— where everything was so natural, not a bit forced association. . . . I look at them with a more appreciative eye. I believe I would accept them more. Formerly when I talked to a colored person, I was aware he was colored. Now I do not, probably because it is no longer unusual. . . . We needed both week-ends. . . . The personal contacts were better than the speeches.

On the second test I was probably more lenient, more broad, simply because you realize a whole lot of them are just as good as you are. Instead of saying Never, I said Some. I would accept one as room-mate where I wouldn't have before. . . . I resented it when ———— [a professor in class] burst out with the remark, "I don't like them!"

[Ten months later.] My interest has not abated in the least. . . . I think it one of the most interesting and instructive experiences which I have had in my . . . years in New York. I notice particularly my quickened interest in Negro articles, or Negro playwrights and poets.

A case below the mean, rising to a fairly high score, and dropping slightly.

It seemed strange to have them in class. I had never talked with any before this year. At ———— was the first time I had ever shaken hands with them or eaten with them. I had never been in a Negro home. It seemed very novel. It was my first time in a Negro church. I felt those people were my equal. It gave me a realization of what contributions they have made to literature, to poetry. It made me realize they have been the oppressed race. They haven't been given the privileges we have, although sometimes they are more able than we are. . . . I didn't see any reason why they shouldn't have the same privileges. . . . On the second test I think I changed, but I don't consciously know how. On the second test I was probably more honest. We had more subject matter to go on.

[Ten months later.] My attitude toward them remains the same as last spring. . . . Many people do not feel the same way about them that we do, but in many instances have seen things differently when we have related some of our experiences and impressions.

A case with low score, rising well above, and ending at, the mean.

I am remaking my attitudes. . . . Formerly when a Negro sat down beside me on the subway, something jumped, but since Harlem that hasn't happened. . . . I have told———— I am a changed person. . . . It was a tremendous change for me in two short week-ends. . . . I am uncertain whether I changed my score.

[Ten months later.] That is one great shining light in my year at Teachers College. However, I have slipped back into my Southern routine, thus failing to have any contacts. . . . Perhaps that may cause a little change in me, I hope not.

A case with low score, rising above the mean, and ending below it.

I was a little worried about it in the beginning before going on the trip. After I had met a few of them, I felt differently. I was pleased that I didn't have to eat with them the first Sunday. By the next Saturday I had gotten over it. . . . I felt a little uneasiness at going into ———, . . . but felt quite at ease because ——— was such a pleasant personality. . . . One thing that helped me was going with ——— from ——— where they are over racial prejudice. . . . I have gotten over the little squeamish feeling I had before. . . . I have no idea whether I answered the same way or not, and I had no idea why the test was given twice.

[Ten months later.] As to my reactions, the ones that stand out most clearly are, first, their striking similarity to adolescent boys and girls, in spite of the fact that in this adolescent group I found many individuals much older and wiser than I. Even their attitude toward the white race was similar to a growing child's attitude toward their elders, a sort of sublime faith if the elder proved kind, and bitter resentment if the elder were unjust. Secondly, the question of intermarriage. Frankly, I was shocked at their candor, expressing themselves to be not only willing, but eager, for a white marriage. For their part I cannot blame. On the white man's side, as most children are easy to love and the Negro has so many childlike qualities, the possibility of a love affair is acute. Theoretically, the mixture of the races might be a good thing. But in practise No. It violates traditions and principles, and I could not help feeling toward any one who made such a union as I would toward a traitor.

A case below the mean, rising to a high score, and ending moderately high.

——— you would remember longest. You could see what the race problem was to some one striving for the same thing you are. . . . It was the first time I was ever in a Negro home. On the first test I was against taking a Negro into my own home. . . . During the fall we had been arguing whether Negro homes were clean. The homes were in fine taste. . . . The discovery of different levels among Negroes as with us was the most important result of the seminar. . . .

On the second test I felt I should show some improvement. . . .
I moved from None to Few, probably changed on Negro guest at
theater, Negro guest in home, probably not so much on living,
wouldn't like to have them in neighborhood. I felt a shift of feeling at the Dunbar Apartments.

[Ten months later.] Perhaps unconsciously there is an attempt
on my part to be more receptive to the Negro students in my
classes. . . . In discussions of the racial problem . . . I do find that
I ally myself on the side of the Negro much more definitely than
before. . . . Frankly, I do not think that the underlying feelings or
prejudices of many individuals in the group were materially altered.
No doubt it brought more forcibly to the attention the factor of
individual differences in operation among the Negro race as well
as the white race. . . . It may be that the type of person who accepted
the opportunity to enter the Harlem Seminar was in itself a selec-
tive factor, and . . . that they were more naive and fluctuating than
the typical Teachers College student.

A case somewhat above the mean, rising to a high score, and
ending moderately high.

A good many of us had the preconceived idea that the Negro
could only do lesser things. . . . Its value was to confirm the fact
that the Negro had possibilities, that he wasn't always meant to be
a porter and do the menial tasks of life, people who need to have
musical and literary abilities developed.

I feel very strongly about the mixing of the races, intermarrying. It's all right to have friends and business associations. I draw
the line at intermarriage.

I was more interested in the second test. . . . I didn't consciously make any changes.

A case with low score, going moderately high, and dropping
slightly.

I was indoctrinated with the idea that Negroes couldn't do
things, just didn't have brains, culture. . . . Too bad, but nothing
I could do anything about. . . . I'm in a purely Southern organization. . . . I had had no contact with educated Negroes. I had never
had any experience as guest, I never before attended a Negro
church. . . . If I were to summarize it, I would probably say that
the whole trip had been purely educational, that I learned a whole
lot of things I didn't know before, and that I had developed a de-

cidedly greater feeling of brotherhood to the people as a race. I notice that whenever I come in contact with them, I feel a very great interest in them. . . . Formerly I felt it's just too bad they are like that. I think I'd try to see to it that they have their chance. I probably wouldn't go out and pioneer, but when the occasion comes up for discussion, I would express my opinion, and it would be a much more decided opinion than before. . . . I knew that the reason I was inconsistent [on the first test] was public opinion. I realized . . . that I had changed my scores . . . I debated for some time whether to go or not.

[Ten months later.] I believe that I meet them more as if they were of my own race, that is, more naturally than before.

A case at the mean, rising to a high score, and hardly dropping.

The talks stood out because I learned most from them. . . . I had never met on a social level intellectual classes of Negroes. . . . I was irritated by a couple of speeches I liked best. I don't blame them for being bitter, but wonder if it's the right attitude. . . . I liked the groups in Harlem, but wouldn't accept them everywhere. . . . I didn't meet any of them enough to know whether I'd want to be friends. . . . I don't believe it changed me. . . . Except for being married, I'd accept these relationships in an emergency.

[Ten months later.] I regret I have not had time to pursue the readings I have checked to do as well as to renew contacts made last year. I remember with pleasure many of the contacts . . . and have hoped to get back.

Cases Showing Gain, Later Reduced More Than Half

A case with low score, rising well above the mean, ending below it.

I hadn't shaken hands, hadn't eaten with any, nor been in a Negro home. . . . In ———— I saw the worst side, I never saw the cultured ones. . . . I had felt I was as good as any nigger. Now I'm taken down a peg. . . . Before the seminar I would have read [a church decision in the news calling for equal hotel privileges at church conferences] without thinking about it, now I feel it was a very fine thing. . . . My appreciation of Negroes is going to make me see foreign people differently, that we are all very, very much alike. . . . At the Y.W. I wanted it changed so that *they* would sit with us. . . . I don't feel I have gone through any very striking change . . . but it has made me a little more humble. It broadened me, made me more thoughtful. Formerly my attitude was negative: instead of being decent to some one, I think I would have ignored. . . . I was thrilled at ———. One of the things that struck me most forcibly was the church, so dignified and scholarly. The whole day was a revelation. . . . I have wondered how I would act if I should meet some of these people in company with others who might object; how strong would I be? In the case of ——— and ———, there'd be no question. But if a different type, I'm not certain I'd be as broad as I think I am.

[Ten months later.] The type of contacts we experienced with Negroes last year were on the whole very pleasant. After the first meeting I was scarcely aware of the Negro as such, but I was at all times aware of intensely interesting people whom I recognized as my equals and superiors intellectually.

A case at the mean, rising to a high score, and ending near the mean.

The new thing was meeting in a social way. I met the social problem that I hadn't felt before. I had been perfectly willing to accept previous professional relations. . . . I had no idea they had developed as they had, the writers' group especially. . . . It would be splendid if our [professional group] could have an experience like this. . . . I feel it has changed my attitude very little. It made me aware of the problem, a sort of regret to find an antagonism on their part toward white people. I felt I had missed something by not knowing they had so much to offer. . . . [In subsequent discussions] I felt I was defending a new outlook with new data. . . . I felt more interest in the test a second time, and more willingness to do it because the experiment had been so worthwhile. . . . One reaction: at the time of the tea I had to leave early from an engagement with a Southern friend, who was disgusted—"To go to a nigger tea!"

[Ten months later.] Only contacts have been professional. . . . Knowing of the high incidence of disease . . . perhaps influences my feeling about personal association . . . without knowing health status. In retrospect I think my reactions to the type of contacts experienced in New York City are much the same as to same type of contacts with white people. A few of the persons and contacts stand out as real events. . . . Others impressed me as being very shallow and as following the crowd. This would be true in any group of people.

Both these cases lost all their gains on the Relationship Test.

Cases First Gaining, Then Falling to the Initial Level

A case with very low score, rising somewhat, and falling again.

I was more conscious of things after than before. . . . We don't as a rule have the prejudice that people think we have. There isn't hatred. There are people anywhere that you wouldn't associate with. . . . I went to ———— for training because they didn't admit Negro students. Going there influenced me. . . . I was older and was giving the matter more conscious thought. I wouldn't let them [their presence] deter me from getting what I wanted. . . .

I had a Negro nurse, was very fond of her, called her Mama, she thinks of me as her baby. . . . If she was sick, I would go to her house to look after her . . . but not repeatedly. . . . I think all attitude tests are foolish anyway, they can be answered in so many ways . . . [In respect to individual items] I might be willing to do it one time, but not all the time.

[Ten months later.] I thought it was a novel experience, but I do not care for any repetition. . . . I found that girls of mixed blood were not so disturbing as formerly. . . . This is due to a decision on my part to accept a . . . situation over which I had no control in a way calling for the least expenditure of energy on my part. This is in line with my attitude of accepting all situations in a manner that would help rather than hinder me.

At first stationary, this case gained slightly on the Relationship Test.

A case with high score, rising to the highest, and dropping back.

I hadn't known so many cultured Negroes. . . . The Harlem experience gave two different ways of solving the race problem, the New York and Chicago policies. . . .

[Ten months later.] I recall with a great deal of pleasure my contacts with the Negro in New York, comparing it with that of the Chicago Negro again. I have had as guest in my home my childhood . . . Negro friend. . . . I feel no color barrier.

Part of the gain on the Relationship Test was held.

A case with rather low score, rising to the mean, and falling back.

It has made me think more of the rights of other peoples, other races. Unless one comes in contact . . . , you tend to forget them, not even to think of them. . . . I had felt that in general they were rather inferior. Now I would accept many of them as my superiors. . . . I still find that the whiter they are the more acceptable they are. . . . It opened my eyes to the immense number of Negroes in this country. . . . I don't see any way out except amalgamation, although on the individual basis I don't quite approve. . . . I think the second test a little more favorable,—any points at which I could accept them on an individual basis, as neighbor, travelling companion, etc.

[Ten months later.] So far as I am willing to admit them to social contacts, it is entirely on an individual basis. The first requisite . . . is that they be cultured. . . . The more nearly white they are, the more acceptable they are to me. Their features must not be intensely Negroid. Thick lips and a broad nose are repulsive. . . . I feel that the Negroes with whom we came into contact . . . last year were representative of the highest type in this country. Nearly all of them had a high percentage of white blood. Whether their high status is due to their admixture of white blood or not, I do not know, but I am inclined to think it is an important factor.

A case with moderately high score, rising to high, and falling back.

What I liked was the opportunity to get together two and two. . . . You sort of have a feeling that people who are black must lead a different sort of home life than white people. . . . Though you may be told that not all Negroes are of the peasant type, it's pretty hard to realize it until you see their homes and what they are doing, their standards. . . . Some one said: So-and-So was over in Harlem and didn't see what you saw. Isn't the cream just as typical as the scum?

[Ten months later.] It is a fact that I never "see" the difference in color; and I have heard several other teachers say the same thing [although there are not more than thirty Negroes in the student body of a thousand].

With one exception all cases showing an initial rise in score have now been reported. After dealing with the cases initially stationary, the four cases which ended with lower scores than they began with will be discussed.

Cases with Stationary Score on the First Re-Test

A case with high score, gaining on the second re-test.

My feeling before was negative, neither one thing nor the other. . . . I was surprised at finding there really is a difference among Negroes. . . . My appreciation and understanding deepened . . . with knowledge, just knowledge, of what they had done in music, art, literature, culture in general, and then their kindliness and hospitality. . . . Later I had heated discussion with a friend who wanted to keep Negroes in their place. Probably I wouldn't have argued previously. My viewpoint is not changed perhaps, but defense of it is stronger. . . . I wondered how we were fortunate enough to be invited.

[Ten months later.] Newspaper items concerning Negroes have been read with more interest than before. . . . Though no particular aversion was felt toward Negroes previous to the Harlem visits, they did give me a much broader view of the race problem and established a more sympathetic attitude. They were among the most interesting experiences I had during my one year in New York City.

A case at the mean on all three tests.

The whole thing was a surprise . . . I forgot my aversion by being in the group. I didn't have it by the time we were at the Y.W. I wouldn't have missed this experience. . . . I feel a different attitude to those in my classes. . . . I gained some understanding of the whole situation down here in Harlem. I hadn't thought very highly of it, thought it something to be avoided. . . . I hadn't even thought of their having done anything before. . . . In the first test I had a feeling of conflict. I probably answered better than I would act. The second test was probably a better gauge. I probably didn't change my responses. I still had a feeling of conflict. This is one thing that is going to stand out this year.

[Ten months later.] Did you once tell us that . . . [probably] we would [some day] think "before Harlem" and "after Harlem"?

. . . To me, the two week-ends spent . . . in Harlem constitute one of the highest spots of the year I spent in New York City. I wouldn't exchange them for any other single experience. . . . I have come to think of those more informal contacts we had as of greater value than the more formal types we experienced. For example, I should not now vote the lectures we heard above our visits to homes, playgrounds, etc., where we had an opportunity to talk with people, and to know what many of them were thinking and feeling and doing.

A case with moderately high score on two tests. No third test.

I was quite surprised to see the freedom here. . . . It was very interesting to me to hear those brilliant people speaking. . . . It has given me an entirely different idea of Negro life and the possibilities of the Negro. . . . A real change. Now I look at them twice.

Four Cases Ending Below Initial Score

A case with moderately low score, dropping somewhat, and recovering part of loss to end 18 points lower.

I didn't know Negroes had things like that . . . I got a real thrill out of ———. I went into the kitchen and offered to help. Well, I surprised myself. . . . I got a huge thrill out of the poetry of Langston Hughes. White people are touching the social problem. He certainly did that in "Waldorf Astoria." . . . ———'s talk annoyed me, upset me. I have had ingrained in me the idea of just giving them opportunities, instead of amalgamation. I thought ——— personally was delightful. ——— didn't annoy me, perhaps because I was now used to it. . . . It's new that they do think it's coming [amalgamation]. . . . We are accustomed to Negroes living in an off place, where nothing happens. . . . It made me wish all colored people could have a Harlem. . . . One thing I liked was the way they treated us. Many people would resent us, or be overly nice. They took us in as friends. . . . I've always been troubled about eating with them, but when ——— spoke, we all hoped Miss ——— would sit with us. If ——— [another admired personality] came to my home town, I've tried my best to decide what I'd do. I'd probably go to one of the colored teachers and ask for accommodations. . . . I probably didn't change a lot [on the test]. I probably changed to More than Few on eating. I probably felt dubious about entertaining. Yet I thought: if that isn't a dirty deal; they entertain me, and I not them.

[Ten months later.] [After the lynching] all of the Negroes left town, but many had moved back, and we had a Sunday dinner in the home of one of them . . . where even the President of the college ate. . . . I was rather disturbed at the number of Negroes [at a recent church entertainment in another state]. . . . I feel keenly interested in the people we met there [in Harlem] and in their activities. I am following the Harlem Hospital investigation . . . and was pleased to note the names of two men whom we knew. . . . Hearing —— reminded me of Paul Robeson, whom I consider one of the most human artists I have ever met. . . . I am glad I had the privilege of meeting those people, but I still believe in segregation.

A case somewhat above the mean, dropping slightly below the mean, and remaining stationary 40 points below initial score.

My idealism I had built up about the Negro was rudely shocked [during the war], probably due to so many of them crowding up so suddenly. . . . The stevedores were not very ambitious, and I had a feeling that they should have been in the service. . . . I think this Harlem trip did me good. . . . [Outstanding Negro students at Teachers College] made me realize that there are outstanding persons of the Negro race, and that's to my mind the most important factor in improving interracial relations because most people think there is just one type in the Negro race. . . . Right at the first moment I was pleased with the broadminded attitude of —— to stand up and admit shortcomings of the Negro race. I had never heard a Negro talk about interracial relations. . . . I do feel that the sermon by —— compared favorably with any sermon I ever heard, one of the first ten or fifteen. . . . I don't think I ever had the Southern attitude, either the affection or the hatred. After maturity by reading I felt the Negro's condition in the South, and felt it wasn't justified, but all the while I had in the back of my mind the picture of the Negroes sitting around on South Street in the sun. . . .

I felt the test didn't give an accurate picture of my attitude toward the Negro. . . . I felt a little disgusted at the type of test. I felt that anything I put down wouldn't register my feelings in the matter. On the second test my feelings were intensified. . . . I didn't associate the Harlem experience with the test, even the second test. I hadn't considered it as an experimental procedure, and it was something of a surprise when I learned it. . . . Another thing at the time that was a little disconcerting to me was that it might be embarrassing to the Negroes in the class. Up to this year I had always thought that interracial problems were problems for the white man, not for the Negro,—didn't need to have them around when you were discussing them. I thought it might be embarrassing to such a man as ———, but obviously it wasn't. . . . There is no doubt I feel much more liberal toward the Negro.

A case with moderately low score, rising to the mean, and then falling to a very low score 52 points below the starting point.

What stood out was the feeling that they were oppressed. Why do they play on that so much? . . . It was a new experience living with them. Where there are families in ———, there is no question of social relations. . . . I think of them as a nation, or a people detached from ourselves, with whom there should not be too much mingling socially. . . . As for intermarrying, I don't believe in that. . . . I had a feeling of the jungle when I saw him. . . . ——— emphasized suffering most [in his sermon]. I felt that [he] felt he had been oppressed himself. . . . I think the whole thing hinges on the individual. I feel it was a pity they ever came here. . . . The trip broadened my knowledge. I hadn't realized before what Harlem meant in different classes of society. . . . I felt an objection to taking the first test. I may have changed on the second test. Going to a home or a dance I probably marked Yes on the second. I would be broadminded enough to do this.

[Ten months later.] I am quite in sympathy with educating the Negro. However, I believe it will be better for humanity if their social contacts are confined within their own race. Social contacts invariably lead to intermarriage, and that is one point of which I strongly disapprove with regard to the Negro. I enjoyed last year's contacts with the Negro people, more as an educational venture than as an experience I could hope to have repeated daily. I felt that the people we visited were much above the average type, and this was due in no small measure to the high percentage of white ancestry. This may sound rather prejudiced in comparison with my attitude at the time last year. This is not because I have any aversion to the Negro as an individual, but as far as *I* am concerned, I am not interested in seeking them out as my friends, but I can still appreciate what they may be able to achieve themselves.

A case with high score, dropping successively to moderately high and then to the mean, 88 points below the starting point.

In a way it's a bad thing to have ———. ——— did more to arouse a feeling of prejudice than anything. There was very little before, but this aroused it. [So-and-So] did the same. . . . This was the first time I had contact with Negroes on a social basis. I had never been in a Negro church, or a Negro home, nor had I eaten with Negroes. . . . A chance to exchange ideas on terms of social equality is very important. It was a chance to realize the very great differences there are between Negroes. I knew it intellectually before, but didn't realize it. This was a chance to see through their eyes, to realize the extent of their bitterness. . . . It is much more difficult than one thinks in advance to make these social friendships.

I answered the questions much more liberally than I really felt. I had a defensive attitude toward people I regarded as down-and-out. I tried to make the second test as nearly like the first as possible, but couldn't remember it all. In a sense I was a little more honest the second time, on the other hand the problem is hopeless. The test didn't get at something vital in my feeling. The essence isn't whether you will travel, eat, or room. It is the feeling toward the whole race as a problem. I have a much more hopeless feeling toward its solution. . . . Perhaps it's better to make a distinct . . . break. . . . I appreciate variety in color as never before. . . . When you think of these people as individuals, I'd be just as friendly as possible.

[Ten months later, reports various contacts.] I feel I am fairly broadminded on the subject, but still have some little prejudice.

Now that reports from all members of the seminar have been given, the reader can judge how nearly the interviews and the tests tend to agree. That there is fair approximation does not seem open to doubt, and the degree of the approximation may indicate the degree of the test's validity.

Outcomes of the Experience

So far as evidence is available, the results of the Harlem experience, as indicated during the subsequent year, were for the most part inner, rather than overt. They consisted in re-orientation of feeling and attitude, and in a new mind-set toward

Negroes and Negro problems. For the most part there was little concrete action. In the aggregate there was a good deal of reading, considerable private discussion, some increase in cordiality to Negro students and workers. There were a few gestures of hospitality. A few individuals visited Harlem again, but without developing the personal contacts of the seminar. Three or four students utilized their experience in college essays and reports, and one or two in public addresses on Negro literature and culture given in their home communities. An interesting spontaneous proposal to bring a Southern professional group into touch with some of the leading personalities of the seminar during their winter residence in the South apparently was shelved. The clearest case of individual development in terms of decreased social distance was a student who participated in a number of Negro intellectual and social activities. The educational experiment with Southern high school students seems to stand alone as an outcome with immediate social outreach.

A number of reasons can be suggested for this paucity of overt results. Sixteen of the group were still engaged in their graduate studies. Among those at work in all parts of the country some were in communities where Negroes are rare. This is not to underrate mere personal interpretation of the Negro in such areas, if a national awareness of the Negro's part in American life is to develop. Some were in communities where custom rigidly restricts Negro-white relationships, and where normal inertia is reinforced by public opinion. Other illustrations could doubtless be found to indicate that the appropriate stimuli were absent or too weak, or the circumstances too unpropitious, to produce responses in terms of the new readiness created by the experiment. It is conceivable that more outcomes would appear if experiences of this kind were integrated into the individuals' curricula of educational experience as a whole. At a time of renewed plasticity, when old stereotypes were weakened, and interest was focused, provision of thorough study and discussion of the many issues of fact and opinion which had been brought to consciousness might be expected to eventuate in well-scrutinized convictions and purposes of the most intelligent and appropriate kind. One member of the seminar, in a letter written soon after its close, said:

> If such trips are to be used educationally, I feel that a follow-up discussion is necessary, wherein under expert guidance, students might be able to distinguish certain trends.

This was of course outside the terms of the present experiment, but might be regarded as plausible, and could even be investigated experimentally.

VI: Summary and Conclusion

THE present experiment represents, so far as could be ascertained, the first scientific attempt to measure the effects on attitudes toward the Negro produced by cultural contacts with outstanding Negro individuals and groups in their own community. Contacts of this sort are occasionally employed inside or outside academic circles in the belief that they promote more favorable attitudes toward the Negro, and proposals are sometimes made that a fuller use of such first-hand experiences in education should be undertaken by properly located institutions.

In measuring the effectiveness of these influences a controlled experiment was carried out in which students of education were exposed to intellectual and social contacts of various kinds with leading people of Negro Harlem. At the outset, in order to provide scientific measures of attitude changes, (1) a battery of tests of attitude toward the Negro, composed in part of current tests already validated and in part of tests of social distance specially constructed for this investigation, was administered to 354 students of Teachers College, Columbia University. (2) Without reference to the test or the experimental purpose, an experimental group of 46 students was obtained by invitation through the mail, and exposed for four days (two consecutive week-ends) to a variety of contacts graduated and integrated to facilitate easy emotional and social adjustments to Negroes. (3) A control group of 46 students, closely paired by individual scores and approximately comparable in age, sex, and geographical origin, was likewise established. (4) About ten days after the Harlem experiences all the classes previously tested, from which the experimental and control groups were drawn, were re-tested on the same test battery. The test battery was found to have a re-test reliability of .92 based on 219 cases, and on the initial test of 354 cases the various sub-tests of the battery were found to have fairly high correlations with the total, and fairly low correlations with one another. It was a surprise to discover a correlation of only .52 between the presumably comparable forms of the Thurstone-Hinckley test, and of the two, Form B appeared to be both the more reliable and the more discriminating measuring instrument. (5) Two months or more after the re-test individual interviews with members of the experimental group on a series of questions covering individual histories, impressions of the Harlem experiences, and outcomes, contributed supplementary evidence of the effect of the experiment on individual attitudes. (6) Ten months or more after the re-test a second re-test was administered by mail to the experimental and control groups to measure the degree of permanence of the experimental effects.

Results

1. Marked increases in favorable attitude toward the Negro were registered by the experimental group. While on the first re-test the mean scores of the control group remained practically constant, statistically significant increases in the mean scores of the experimental group appeared on all parts of the test battery except one; in the total score this increase over the control group, divided by its standard error, amounted to 7.36, a highly significant gain, and even the part registering lowest gain over the control group obtained a quotient of 2.89, closely approximating statistical significance.

2. While little correlation was found between initial attitude scores of 354 students and either age or intelligence, there was a strong tendency for men to be more favorable than women. With age the correlation was .04, with intelligence .13, in respect to sex the difference in favor of the men divided by its standard error was 2.66, which approaches statistical reliability. Students

brought up in the South had the lowest mean score, but sectional differences were in no case statistically significant. In the experimental group students below the mean age, and students below the mean score, gained the more, and women gained slightly more than men. Differential gains according to geographical environment in youth were slight. None of these differences in gain were statistically significant.

3. Initial interest, expressed in the fact that members of the experimental group volunteered for the experiences, appeared to be of minor importance compared with the influence of the experiences themselves. Twenty-three cases of volunteers unable eventually to attend were studied as an "interested control group," individually paired with experimental group cases. In comparison with this group, only half as large, the mean gain of the small experimental group was even larger than in the original experimental–control group comparison, and the difference divided by the standard error of the difference for the total was still high, 5.92.

4. After a lapse of eleven months from the exposure a high persistence of gain was found. Comparing 40 of the original pairs, the difference between the original and the second re-test mean for the total, when divided by its standard error, amounted to 4.74, and was statistically significant on three of the five subtests. Moreover, the losses were concentrated in a few special cases, and 25 members of the experimental group kept all their original gains or increased them.

The interviews indicated that extreme losses were due to definite causes, such as discovery of basic issues on which a negative choice was preferred, irritation at characteristics of the test battery, or deliberate responses on the first test more favorable than attitudes actually held.

5. Analysis of original shifts of attitude on particular attitude statements produced impressive results. Categorical barriers against Negroes in a number of personal relationships were

abandoned by highly significant percentages of the experimental group. Among the relationships now acceptable on certain terms to largely increased percentages of the experimental group were those of dining at the same table, sharing the same stateroom, accepting as principal in the same school, entertaining as guest at a white dance, accepting as escort at the theater, as host at a Negro dance, or as intimate chum. These relationships were among those found absolutely unacceptable not only to a majority of the total group of 354 students, but also to a majority of the experimental group at the beginning of the experiment. Significant percentages also changed from approval to disapproval of segregation, and registered enhanced respect for Negro abilities. The marked change in those attitudes which might be supposed to be emotionally most firmly held as shown by greatest initial objection by the group to the series of personal relationships can best be explained in terms of a greatly enhanced valuation of at least certain Negroes as persons, and a new expectation that certain Negroes might be acceptable in relationships where qualities of personality peculiarly count. The same trend was evident in other large shifts of opinion within the experimental group having somewhat lower indices of significance. In fact, at the end of the experiment only two of the relationships presented, kinship by marriage and marriage itself, were totally unacceptable to a majority of the experimental group, though it had started out in fairly close agreement with public opinion in the total group. Incidentally, this evidence tends to support the notion of a group factor in attitudes toward the Negro, susceptible to the influences inherent in certain types of personal contact, and to weaken the notion of complete specificity of attitudes.

These indications from the test results received considerable corroboration from interviews obtained two months later. The discovery of superior personalities in an unexpected quarter tended to provoke a revaluation of the Negro, and the graduated procedure of the seminar led in many cases to conscious release from infantile fears and inhibitions. Both the tests and the interviews point to individual changes of feeling and attitude accomplished in a much shorter time than is usually expected. This suggests a lag in development which could be quickly overcome under proper conditions. Every traveler is familiar with the swift enlightenment and re-orientation which may take place on exposure to significant new data, and social distance apparently acts like geographical isolation prior to new experience.

6. The interviews tend to validate the test results, and indicate not only intellectual gains from the experiences, but consciousness of emotional readjustments toward Negroes which in numerous cases were rapid enough to surprise the subjects themselves. While these inner changes seem to have been quite real and in most cases permanent, their result in action of social significance seems to have been rare, though a few reports a year later point to very interesting exceptions.

Bearing on Education

First-hand experience of the cultural life of a socially distant group like the Negro represents a curriculum value of importance not only intellectually but emotionally. Readjustments of attitudes promoting a higher valuation of persons and contributing directly to the psychological foundation needed for genuine democracy may be effected in a relatively short time under appropriate conditions through the influences inherent in personal contact with outstanding individuals and groups in their own community. What is necessary are the properly integrated stimuli hitherto deficient. These should form a compact, unified body of experiences rising gradually and cumulatively from the less difficult to the initially more difficult social contacts. Such experiences not only provide basic thought-provoking data to serve as fundamental points of reference for future thinking, but provide simultaneously situations in which new adjustments of greater emotional and social maturity seem easy and plausible. While such integration of influences and responses within the limited period of exposure can produce genuine inner changes of attitude toward a group, integration of such units of experiences in a larger educational Gestalt of the curriculum as a whole which might capitalize the new plasticity and interest might conceivably lead to more deliberate and purposeful outcomes of much greater social value.

Bibliography

1. ALLPORT, G. W. and VERNON, P. E. "The Field of Personality." *Psychological Bulletin,* 27:677-730, 1930.
2. BAIN, R. "Theory and Measurement of Attitudes and Opinions." *Psychological Bulletin,* 27:357-379, 1930.
3. BIDDLE, W. W. *Propaganda and Education.* Contributions to Education, No. 531. Bureau of Publications, Teachers College, Columbia University, New York, 1932.
4. BUSCH, H. M. "Race Attitudes in Children." *Religious Education,* 21:277-281, 1926.
5. CHICAGO COMMISSION ON RACE RELATIONS. *The Negro in Chicago.* The University of Chicago Press, 1922.
6. COE, G. A. Unpublished lecture notes.
7. DEWEY, JOHN. "Race Prejudice and Friction." *Chinese Political and Social Science Review* (Peking), 6:1-17, 1924.
8. "Each According to His Own Experience," by Ruml, Beardsley. Unpublished lecture before the Social Science Research Council, September 2, 1930.
9. HARPER, M. H. *Social Beliefs and Attitudes of American Educators.* Contributions to Education, No. 294. Bureau of Publications, Teachers College, Columbia University, New York, 1927.
10. HARRIS, A. J., RENNERS, H. H., and ELLISON, C. E. "The Relation between Liberal and Conservative Attitudes in College Students and Other Factors." *Journal of Social Psychology,* 3:320-37, 1932.
11. HINCKLEY, E. D. "The Influence of Individual Opinion on Construction of an Attitude Scale." *Journal of Social Psychology,* 3:283-296, 1932. (See also his unpublished Ph.D. dissertation, University of Chicago.)
12. HINCKLEY, E. D. *The Measurement of Social Attitudes.* Scale No. 3, Attitude Toward the Negro. The University of Chicago Press, 1930.
13. HUNTER, C. W. "A Comparative Study of the Relationship Existing Between the White Race and the Negro Race in the State of North Carolina and in the City of New York." Master's Essay, Columbia University, 1927.
14. LASKER, B. *Race Attitudes in Children.* New York, Henry Holt and Co., 1929.
15. LIKERT, R. *A Technique for the Measurement of Attitudes.* Archives of Psychology No. 140. Columbia University, New York, 1932.

16. MAY, M. A., HARTSHORNE, H., and WELTY, R. E. "Personality and Character Tests." *Psychological Bulletin*, 25:422-43, 1928.

17. MURPHY, G. and MURPHY, L. B. *Experimental Social Psychology*. Harper and Brothers, New York, 1931.

18. NATIONAL EDUCATION ASSOCIATION, DEPARTMENT OF SUPERINTENDENCE. *Character Education*. Tenth Yearbook. The Association, Washington, D. C., 1932.

19. PETERSON, R. and THURSTONE, L. L. *Motion Pictures and the Social Attitudes of Children*. The Macmillan Company, New York, 1933.

20. PINTNER, R. "Neurotic Tendency and Its Relation to Some Other Mental Traits." *School and Society*, 36:765-767, 1932.

21. PRESIDENT'S RESEARCH COMMITTEE ON SOCIAL TRENDS. *Recent Social Trends in the United States*. McGraw-Hill Book Co., New York, 1933.

22. SCHLORFF, P. W. "An Experiment in the Measurement and Modification of Racial Attitudes in School Children." Unpublished Ph.D. dissertation, New York University, 1930.

23. THURSTONE, L. L. "A Law of Comparative Judgment." *Psychological Review*, 34:273-296, 1927.

24. THURSTONE, L. L. "The Measurement of Change in Social Attitude." *Journal of Social Psychology*, 2:230-235, 1931.

25. WANGER, R. "High School Study of the Negro and His Problems." *High School Teacher*, 8:104-106, 1932.

26. WATSON, G. "Tests of Personality and Character." *Review of Educational Research*, 2:183-270, 1932.

27. WATSON, G. "Wholes and Parts in Education." *Teachers College Record*, 34:119-133, 1932.

28. BAKER, PAUL E. *Negro-White Adjustment*. Association Press, New York, 1934.

Appendix I

THE TEST BATTERY

PART I

A STUDY IN SOCIAL ATTITUDES

Attitudes Toward Negroes in America

Name...................... Local address......................
Institution .... Date...............................

Directions: Negroes in America are associated in a variety of ways with different individuals and groups in the life around them. The following statements cover a wide range of these possible relationships. Certain of the relationships stated may be acceptable to many people, others perhaps to a few or none. In each case consider your own attitude toward the relationship stated and encircle that response which most nearly represents the conditions, if any, under which the relationship would be personally acceptable to you.

Bear in mind differences in color, education, or social position if these affect your decision. There are no "right" answers. Each person will answer differently. Simply try to be as accurate as possible.

Example

	you are personally	
If under *most* conditions	willing to admit a Negro to residence in your home town	encircle MOST
If under *many* conditions	" " " " " " " "	encircle MANY
If under *some* conditions	" " " " " " " "	encircle SOME
If under *few* conditions	" " " " " " " "	encircle FEW
If under *no* conditions	" " " " " " " "	encircle NO

Work carefully but rapidly. Do not delay too long over any one item. If in doubt *underline* that answer which seems most nearly correct. Be sure to answer each item.

I am personally willing to admit a Negro to the following relationships to myself ... *under* MOST, MANY, SOME, FEW, NO *conditions.*

1	Resident	same town	MOST	MANY	SOME	FEW	NO
2		same neighborhood	MOST	MANY	SOME	FEW	NO
3		same street	MOST	MANY	SOME	FEW	NO
4		same hotel	MOST	MANY	SOME	FEW	NO
5		same apartment house	MOST	MANY	SOME	FEW	NO
6		same family as guest	MOST	MANY	SOME	FEW	NO
7		room mate	MOST	MANY	SOME	FEW	NO
8	Traveler	same train	MOST	MANY	SOME	FEW	NO
9		same section of car	MOST	MANY	SOME	FEW	NO
10		adjoining seat	MOST	MANY	SOME	FEW	NO
11		same sleeping car	MOST	MANY	SOME	FEW	NO
12		same restaurant	MOST	MANY	SOME	FEW	NO
13		same table	MOST	MANY	SOME	FEW	NO
14		same class on boat	MOST	MANY	SOME	FEW	NO
15		same stateroom on boat	MOST	MANY	SOME	FEW	NO

I am personally willing to admit a Negro to the following relationships to myself . . . under MOST, MANY, SOME, FEW, NO, *conditions.*

16	Worker	unskilled (in my employ)	MOST	MANY	SOME	FEW	NO
17		skilled (in my employ)	MOST	MANY	SOME	FEW	NO
18		my personal servant	MOST	MANY	SOME	FEW	NO
19		my secretary	MOST	MANY	SOME	FEW	NO
20		member of my professional group or organization	MOST	MANY	SOME	FEW	NO
21		my competitor	MOST	MANY	SOME	FEW	NO
22		my business partner	MOST	MANY	SOME	FEW	NO
23		my superior	MOST	MANY	SOME	FEW	NO
24	Fellow	at my school	MOST	MANY	SOME	FEW	NO
25	student	in my classes	MOST	MANY	SOME	FEW	NO
26		in my study circle	MOST	MANY	SOME	FEW	NO
27		elected a leader	MOST	MANY	SOME	FEW	NO
28		participant in student parties	MOST	MANY	SOME	FEW	NO
29		partner in dance	MOST	MANY	SOME	FEW	NO
30		member of my social set	MOST	MANY	SOME	FEW	NO
31	Pupil	in class I teach	MOST	MANY	SOME	FEW	NO
32	Teacher	at school where I teach	MOST	MANY	SOME	FEW	NO
33		my principal	MOST	MANY	SOME	FEW	NO
34	Church	my denomination	MOST	MANY	SOME	FEW	NO
35	member	branch of my local church	MOST	MANY	SOME	FEW	NO

36		my local church	MOST	MANY	SOME	FEW	NO
37		my social group at church	MOST	MANY	SOME	FEW	NO
38	Citizen	receiving inferior public service (in schools, public works etc.); no vote	MOST	MANY	SOME	FEW	NO
39		equal service; no vote	MOST	MANY	SOME	FEW	NO
40		equal treatment plus vote	MOST	MANY	SOME	FEW	NO
41		lesser official	MOST	MANY	SOME	FEW	NO
42		official of high rank	MOST	MANY	SOME	FEW	NO
43	Friend	protégé	MOST	MANY	SOME	FEW	NO
44		cordial public (no private or social) contacts	MOST	MANY	SOME	FEW	NO
45		my guest at home	MOST	MANY	SOME	FEW	NO
46		my guest at theater	MOST	MANY	SOME	FEW	NO
47		my guest at white dance	MOST	MANY	SOME	FEW	NO
48		my host at Negro home	MOST	MANY	SOME	FEW	NO
49		my escort at theater	MOST	MANY	SOME	FEW	NO
50		my escort at Negro dance	MOST	MANY	SOME	FEW	NO
51		my intimate chum	MOST	MANY	SOME	FEW	NO
52		my kin by marriage	MOST	MANY	SOME	FEW	NO
53		husband or wife	MOST	MANY	SOME	FEW	NO

States in which you resided up to twenty years of age and number of years in each:

. . . .

. . . .

PART II

THURSTONE-HINCKLEY TEST OF ATTITUDE TOWARD THE NEGRO

FORMS A AND B

These tests, prepared by E. D. Hinckley, are in the well-known Thurstone Series on the Measurement of Social Attitudes. Each form comprises sixteen statements to be checked for agreement, disagreement, or uncertainty.

These tests are copyrighted, and permission to reproduce in this study could not be obtained. Copies may be purchased from The University of Chicago Press.

PART III

ITEMS FROM THE MURPHY–LIKERT TEST

Section I: After each question encircle "yes" or "no"; or if you are un-decided or are not sure you understand the question encircle the "?".

1. Would most Negroes, if not held in their places become officious, overbearing, and disagreeable? YES ? NO
2. If you went into a cafeteria in a northern town, sat down, and then realized that you were at the table with a Negro, would you leave the table? YES ? NO
3. Would you shake hands with a Negro? YES ? NO
4. Do you disapprove of the use of the term "nigger"? YES ? NO
5. If you heard of a Negro who had bought a home or a farm, would you be glad? YES ? NO

Section II: In each of the following you are given a preliminary statement which can be completed or answered in any one of five ways. Check whichever of the five most clearly approximates your own opinion.

1. In a community in which the Negroes outnumber the whites, under what circumstances is the lynching of a Negro justifiable?

    ( ) Never
    ( ) In very exceptional cases where a specially brutal crime against a white person calls for swift punishment
    ( ) As a punishment for any brutal crime against a white person
    ( ) As a punishment for any gross offense (felony or extreme in-solence) against a white person
    ( ) As punishment for any act of insolence against a white person

2. In a community where the Negroes outnumber the whites, a Negro who is insolent to a white man should be:

    ( ) excused or ignored
    ( ) reprimanded
    ( ) fined and jailed
    ( ) not only fined and jailed but given corporal punishment (whip-ping, etc.)
    ( ) lynched

Section III: The following list of sentences is in the form of statements of what should or should not be done. If you strongly approve of the statement as it stands, underscore the words "strongly approve," and so on, with regard to the attitudes (approve, undecided, disapprove, strongly dis-approve).

Appendix

1. All Negroes, being in one class, should be treated in about the same way.

Strongly approve
Approve
Undecided
Disapprove
Strongly disapprove

2. Negro homes should be segregated from those of white people.

Strongly approve
Approve
Undecided
Disapprove
Strongly disapprove

3. Where there is segregation, the Negro section should have the same equipment in paving, water, and electric light facilities as are found in the white districts.

Strongly approve
Approve
Undecided
Disapprove
Strongly disapprove

4. If the same preparation is required, the Negro teacher should receive the same salary as the white.

Strongly approve
Approve
Undecided
Disapprove
Strongly disapprove

5. Practically all American hotels should refuse to admit Negroes.

Strongly approve
Approve
Undecided
Disapprove
Strongly disapprove

6. No Negro should be deprived of the franchise except for reasons which would also disenfranchise a white man.

Strongly approve
Approve
Undecided
Disapprove
Strongly disapprove

7. In a community of 1,000 whites and fifty Negroes, a drunken Negro shoots and kills an officer who is trying to arrest him. The white population immediately drive all the Negroes out of town. (Comment on action taken)

Strongly approve
Approve
Undecided
Disapprove
Strongly disapprove

8. A Negro should customarily be addressed by the title Mr. (Mrs., Miss)*

Strongly approve
Approve
Undecided
Disapprove
Strongly disapprove

* In the discussion this item is referred to as IV A because it is treated as one of the miscellaneous items.

PART IV

MISCELLANEOUS ITEMS

Read each statement carefully and place a plus (+) sign before each statement with which you agree or endorse; a minus sign (−) before each statement with which you do *not* agree or do not endorse. Mark question mark (?) if you are undecided, or if, for any reason, the statement is not clear.

( ) 1. The Negro race is contributing to American culture through its art.

( ) 2. The Negro's proper place is in manual work.

( ) 3. Negroes are no different, essentially, from other people.

( ) 4. The Negro race will never reach the cultural and intellectual level of the whites.

( ) 5. The recognized leaders of the Negro race are almost invariably persons of mixed blood and the qualities which have made them leaders are derived from their white ancestry.

( ) 6. The doctrine of evolution proves that Negroes and whites should not mate.

( ) 7. Negro and white children should be educated in the same schools.

( ) 8. The Negro has his own unique contribution to make to American life and should be given every opportunity to express himself.

( ) 9. Negroes are inferior to white people in innate capacity.

( ) 10. Colored people are equal to whites in potential ability but have lacked opportunity.

( ) 11. The Negro has no rights that a white man is bound to respect.

( ) 12. Negroes are more prone to commit sexual offense than is the average white man.

( ) 13. Negro children in the public schools are able to do as good work as is done by the average white child of similar age.

( ) 14. Negroes should be accepted now to complete social equality with white persons.

Appendix II

FORM OF INVITATION TO SEMINAR

Teachers College, Columbia University, New York

Your attention is called to an unusual opportunity being offered a small number of Teachers College students for intimate acquaintance with the cultural life of Negro Harlem. Harlem, nearest neighbor to the Columbia hill, is not only the largest Negro city in the world, but also a unique center of creative leadership in Negro America. If you are interested in the educational experience this opportunity provides, you are cordially invited to become a member of the group. Membership is limited to fifty.

The program will occupy parts of the two week-ends of February 27th and March 5th. Exceptional avenues of approach are provided which can seldom recur. After an interpretation of Harlem by Dr. Elmer Carter, editor of *Opportunity* and an outstanding national figure in Negro sociology, friends are providing automobiles for the afternoon to assist the group in seeing the principal institutions and points of interest of the community. At the close of the afternoon Dr. Schomberg, historian and collector of an unusual library of rare Negro manuscripts and books, will discuss and exhibit his collection. The evening will be given over to a program of Negro literature and music.

In the course of the two week-ends there will be addresses by Jessie Fauset, novelist; Ira Reid, sociologist; Dr. Louis Wright, talented surgeon; and others; also a tea with college groups, luncheon with the Social Workers Club, visits to playgrounds, churches, the Harlem Hospital, co-operative apartments, and other important institutions of the community. An informal evening and party at one of the most distinguished homes will provide an opportunity to meet well-known artists and writers such as Countee Cullen, Rose Maclendon, Rudolf Fisher, and others.

Please fill out the enclosed reply card, and mail *at once,* if you are interested in joining the group. Copies of the program in detail will be presented at the organization meeting of the group, *Tuesday, February 23rd, 4 P.M., Room 236, Macy Hall.* If you desire earlier information concerning details of program or arrangements, inquiries may be made on Friday, February 19th, 5–6 P.M., Room 236 Macy. *Expenses:* Carfares and the cost of three or four meals, averaging 50¢ to 75¢ each.

F. Tredwell Smith, *Director, Harlem Seminar*

Vita

FRED TREDWELL SMITH was born in Castleton, Vermont, on June 24, 1894. He received his early education in the vicinity of Boston, and attended college at Harvard, receiving the degree of A.B. in 1915. During the next three years he was a graduate student at Teachers College, Columbia University, and at Union Theological Seminary, receiving the degrees of M.A. and B.D. in 1918. For a year and a half he was a member of the American Persian Relief Commission, working for war refugees near Baghdad, Mesopotamia, in Persia and Transcaucasia. For three years he studied at Oxford University as a Rhodes Scholar, receiving the Oxford B.A. degree in 1922. The following year was spent in further travel and study on the Continent. Subsequent teaching positions were at the American University of Beirut in Syria, the Saidia Lycée of the Egyptian Ministry of Education in Cairo, Franklin and Marshall College, and Teachers College, Columbia University. He taught in the summer school of Hampton Institute in 1927. From 1934 to 1942 he was head of the Social Studies Department of the Dalton School in New York City, and he has returned to this position after a period as consultant on Inter-American Affairs with the Office of Education, Washington, D. C.

Date Due

Due	Returned	Due	Returned
OCT 24 '80			
DEC 5 '80			
JUL 2 0 1988			
JUL 2 6 1986			
APR 1 4 1996	MAR 2 6 1996		
2 4 AUG 1998	AUG 0 4 1998		